OUR ROAD TO DAMASCUS

7 LESSONS FOR A LIFE OF PURPOSE AND MEANING

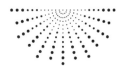

DAN ASSISI

RIVAIL PUBLISHING

First Edition: December 2020

Cover design by Vanessa Mendozzi
Editing by Hannah Kushnick

ISBN 978-1-7359675-2-3 (hard cover)
ISBN 978-1-7359675-0-9 (paperback)
ISBN 978-1-7359675-1-6 (e-book)

Published by Rivail Publishing Company
www.rivailpublishing.com

CONTENTS

To Nicole, David, and Vincent, who remind me of the joys of walking the road every day.

To Paul, whose footprints are so bright we can follow them even at night.

PREFACE

For about a year, I took Paul everywhere I went. We had dinner at the café atop the Tate Modern in London (fittingly overlooking Saint Paul's Cathedral), we drank copious amounts of tea at a quiet plaza in Liberty Station in San Diego, and even dipped our toes in the beautiful blue waters of Nassau together. Everywhere I went, Paul was there in his dusty sandals, patiently waiting for me.

It was supposed to be just an article. Something for people who heard me speak about the road to Damascus at different places throughout the years and had asked me for more. "Do you have this written somewhere?" they would inquire after the talks. When I was hearing the same message from different people in multiple countries, I figured maybe there was something to it. *Maybe,* I thought, *this could be helpful to someone else. Perhaps this can be a chapter of a book that helps us look at old texts with new eyes.* That seemed like an interesting idea. Paul, apparently, had a different one. He kept suggesting more. Fast forward to

12 months later, that short article has become the book you are holding today.

Little did I know that, in the process of writing this book, it would end up helping me rewrite myself. In the midst of it, I decided to leave an organization for which I had worked for 12 years without knowing exactly what was next. I thought about changing careers. I struggled with taking time off. I started a new business. I moved. And, as if all that wasn't change enough, COVID-19 happened. Through it all, no matter whatever else was going on, Paul's lessons still held true. They were still helpful. Little by little, the *article-for-others* had become the *book-for-myself*. The truth is that the time I spent with Paul on the road to Damascus has transformed my life in more ways than one. Much of it was unexpected, but all of it was welcome.

But don't worry: this book is not about my life. It is about a far more interesting one: yours. Whether you go through the whole thing or skip the first chapters to jump straight to the lessons, whether you read it all in one sitting or give yourself time to reflect between sections, whether you use the discussion questions at the end or not, my sincere hope is that some of the joy I experienced writing this book may find you. And that you may find yourself inspired to continue on your own journey to your Damascus—wherever it may lead you.

San Diego, October 26th, 2020

BEFORE WE BEGIN: A WORD ON "RELIGION"

Interpretations of Paul's journey to Damascus abound within Christian traditions. The road to Damascus has, for many, become symbolic of a moment of "conversion" to Christianity: a moment in which a previous "unbeliever" comes in contact with the "Christ" and becomes "Christian." All these words have become loaded in our culture because of their relation to the larger and more complicated "r"-word: "religion." You will not find many of them in this book. The "r"-word itself has evolved over time, and the concept it denotes remains divisive. Even if its original purpose was to bring people together, it can now also immediately push people away. For some, it evokes a context with which they are comfortable; for others, it represents institutions and ways of thinking that they may find limiting or even oppressive. These two groups of people have different definitions of "religion"—and both are right because it is their experience that matters. At the same time, both miss the mark a bit because they are often talking about different things while using the same word. That being the case, confusion and friction follow— exactly what we seek to avoid here. For the sake of clarity, we should untangle this knot before proceeding so you know what you are getting into. Or not getting into.

Let's grab the bull by the horns: what we often call "religion" really is "organized religion." In fact, there is such confusion about the difference between the two that we often think they are one and the same. That's a recipe for disaster. And it gets worse: even people who are keen on organized religion often disagree on which one to choose. Adding insult to injury, sometimes members of a group shut others out because they do not match their specific worldview—in a move often contrary to the very tenets of that religion. So, even if you want to belong to an organized religion, sometimes you are not accepted. It can all be very confusing and hard.

But the word "religion" comes from the Latin word *religare*. *Ligare* comes from connecting, binding together. Much the same way our ligaments often connect two bones in our body, *ligare* is about bringing two different subjects together: you and the divine. Religare, then, is reconnecting individuals to God, the divine, or whatever other word you may choose to employ to describe the guiding force of the cosmos.

The key here is that, by definition, religare is an individual sport: it describes the personal connection each living being has to and with the creator. Each one of us has a one-on-one relationship with G.O.D.—the Guiding, Organizing, Designing force of the universe. Or whatever other nomenclature one chooses. (I myself sometimes use

"Grand Ole Dude" just to throw listeners a curveball and get the conversation going.) The point is: the name doesn't matter—the idea does. Our focus on this book is on concepts and not labels.

Understandably, working on this personal connection with the divine is a difficult thing. Probably for that matter, we have gathered in groups through our common history to work at it together. Talking to each other, we have been able to make better sense of our world. We exchanged ideas and opinions, shared experiences, and made our meaning. With time these groups grew and, as with anything else, required greater organization. Rules, practices and guidelines came about and so did hierarchy. We formalized structures and institutions to accommodate a larger number of people. Today, centuries removed from their origins, we have come to call these groups "religions"—when they should really be more aptly referred to as "organized religions." Therein lies the rub.

No wonder so much friction exists around organized religion and why, in our modern times, more people are struggling to find their place within a context that works for them. Sometimes, to escape it all, we even try to use new words, like "spiritual," to make space and avoid the tangled mess the "r"-word can bring us. Ultimately, we all want to get to the same place but disagree on which road to take. If only we focused on our common destination!

This book is about getting to that destination, about looking at the world through a different lens to allow us to move forward on our journey of meaning and purpose. It is not about picking sides, because it is not a competition. If the structure and fellowship of organized religion work well for you, great: you have found your people and your compass to become a better person. You have your common language and experiences, and this book will not prove difficult to follow—it just may use terms and words that are slightly different than the ones you may be accustomed to in your tradition. For others, who have not found their place within a formal organized religion, who have been scarred by interactions with institutions, or who simply prefer to go it alone, rest assured this book will not box you into anything: it is not about the views of a specific denomination or getting you to join one. You will be able to follow along without the need for any previous context.

In short, this book is not a "religious" one in the sense of "organized religion." It is not anti-religion either. This book is about unpacking a personal experience of an incredible person who decided to change himself—an experience from which we can hopefully transfer some wisdom into our lives. It is a new look into an old story. It invites all of us to leave our preconceived labels and terms aside to focus first on what makes us human: our struggle to grow and find our place in the universe.

On we go, leaving our loaded words behind, as we move to meet Paul on his journey.

1

ON THE ROAD WITH PAUL

"Awake, you that sleep, and arise from the dead, and Christ will shine on you."
(Ephesians 5:14)

These words Paul wrote to a group of early Christians in Ephesus more than 2,000 years ago still echo through the times. They have endured time and space, suffered critique and study, and withstood disdain and adoration to reach us today. It is a simple verse written by a Jewish man in a Roman prison to Gentile friends and acquaintances 840 miles away in what is today Turkey calling them to awaken to a new reality, speaking of a personal transformation so profound that it would cause them to revolutionize how they saw life. His words also spoke of a mysterious figure, the Christ, who remains largely misunderstood to this day and who seemed to possess a light of his own. No doubt, much can be unpacked from these few words. Regardless of whatever personal feelings we may harbor toward them, there is no denying they are full of vigor, vivid imagery, and a sense of urgency and importance.

But are they relevant to us today? Should we listen to them? Who is this Paul person who speaks to us from a distant past and a faraway place? What kind of transformation is this that he promises us? Who truly is this Jesus figure he sees only once in his life and who causes him to change? Is this just a religious experience? How does it relate to us living in a vastly different world than Paul did? What does he know of our challenges and our lives that would lead us to lend him any credence? In short: why would these words matter?

Because Paul's journey to Damascus is the type of voyage of spiritual transformation we all must undertake to truly find our place in this world and our purpose in the universe.

Many of us have already felt it: that there is more to life, to our existence, than we are capable of understanding. We struggle to find happiness, to know where "to go" —yet we sense there is more to it all. But where do we go? And how do we get there? Paul's story may hold some answers. My greatest hope is that these pages may help bridge the time and space between our busy 21st-century lives and the Apostle of the Gentiles two millennia ago— and that they may, ultimately, help you make sense of your own journey to "Damascus."

We would do well to pay attention to Paul and what he has to say as we search for meaning and purpose for our own lives. Saul of Tarsus, eventually to be called Paul, is perhaps one of the greatest examples of personal transformation we have in recorded history. An avid opponent of early Christianity, Paul eventually becomes its greatest exponent—but only after an impromptu encounter with Christ on his way to Damascus. When it happens, he realizes his old habits, his career, and his lifestyle are no longer enough for him. He leaves his successful life behind to do something completely different. In the process, he is abandoned by family and ridiculed by friends, all of whom cannot understand the cause for such change. (Certainly he was mad!) So he starts anew, without truly knowing what lies ahead, and forges on. Eventually, Paul travels on foot through most of the known world at the time—more than once—bringing a message of love and acceptance to all who would hear. By the time he is done with this life, he has sparked new congregations of faith, visited many existing others, personally met and brought hope to thousands of people, mentored a new generation of Christian messengers, befriended and counseled some of Christ's disciples, faced politicians and a Roman emperor, and written letters that have become a central part of Western religious and ethical thinking. More importantly, however, Paul lived a life of fulfillment and purpose.

Such radical change is not for the faint of heart—but it is within our reach. You may have heard of the successful CEO who steps down from their position of power to try something new; of the lawyer who leaves their practice to become a social worker; of the engineer who quits their well-paying job to become a high-school teacher; or of the executive who leaves a successful career behind to become a stay-at-home parent. These stories are as numerous as they are increasingly frequent. And those who undertake such change all have a little bit of Paul in them—we all do. We may think these people have it all, that they have everything that could make them happy and fulfilled—yet clearly something makes them choose to change.

The truth is we are all looking for meaning and purpose. Whether you are a line cook or a CEO, a retail worker or an astronaut, an artist or an engineer, we all at times feel like we are stumbling in the dark, unsure about why we are here and what we should do with our lives. Paul may have some answer for us because he has been there before. He may be able to point us toward the light, to help us awake to a new paradigm that can revolutionize our lives and help us make a dent in the world.

In short, Paul's journey to Damascus can be seen as a symbolic portrayal of the deeply personal and spiritual path we all must trek before finding lasting meaning and purpose for our lives. It is a lot larger than just a religious event. As we relive Paul's experience, we reflect upon our own. As we examine the particulars of his story, we may identify with some of the challenges we face in this life as well as clues as to how to overcome them. That is the wisdom of the Gospel: practical, timeless advice for our daily lives—if we are able to wake up from our spiritual slumber and see ancient places and old names not as curious fiction but as real situations and people who were striving for happiness amid the people they cared about. Just like us.

So, I invite you to get on the road with me toward Damascus. Maybe we will find Paul along the way and, with luck and a little effort, a new philosophy of enlightenment too will shine on us.

2

WHY PAUL?

At first glance, Paul may seem a puzzling choice as a model for the contemporary person looking to find meaning and purpose. After all, what would a Jewish Roman citizen who lived 2,000 years ago know that's relevant to our lives in the 21st century? What kind of advice or insights could he offer us? Things have greatly changed since then: the world is a different place and our lives have a different rhythm. So, then, why Paul?

Simply put, Paul remains one of the most incredible examples of personal transformation we can find in recorded history. Paul's 180-degree turnaround is proof that anyone can change their life, if they are willing. If such a drastic change can be done, we too can accomplish ours.

Standing on this side of history, we often fail to grasp the magnitude of Paul's transformation. The Paul we know today is the Apostle of the Gentiles, the author of 13 out of the 21 letters in the New Testament, the "saint" whose name lends identity to buildings and even cities throughout the world. His figure looms large in the Christian pantheon of heroes. Paul seems otherworldly at times, as if he had been cut from a different cloth to begin with. Yet he was human and flawed, like all of us.

When we come to know of Paul in the modern era, we see the incredible torch-bearer for Christianity but often forget that, before all these accomplishments, he was Saul: one of the most vehement persecutors of the nascent faith. His accomplishments were so many after his change of heart that they blind us to his former reality—when they should instead underscore the difficult transformation he underwent as Saul. In fact, one could argue his accomplishments were so many *because* of his former reality; his drive to contribute to the spiritual development of others was no doubt fueled by a keen and constant awareness of his past doings against the followers of "the Way," as early Christians were known.

In a sense, we could not have had Paul (at least not a Paul as productive as Paul was) without first having Saul. Yes, he took on a new name to symbolize the change he wanted to see in his life: from "Saul," meaning "the greatest," he became "Paul," meaning "the smallest." Nevertheless, he never stopped being Saul. To erase Saul is to shortchange Paul—a lesson we who seek to change ourselves can learn from. Changing ourselves is not about denying our past but, instead, leveraging it to catapult us farther and faster into our future. Who we were has led us to here and now, the necessary starting point to whom we will be. Rather than spending our energy trying to bury a past that does not suit us anymore, we should focus it instead on looking forward, on braving new paths that will lead us to happiness. Much the same way Paul did. After all, driving a car looking only at the rearview mirrors is a recipe for disaster. The good news is we need not worry about erasing our past selves, because in due time they become unrecognizable to those who know our new selves —and to us. After great personal change, our old selves are a distant memory, a mere historical curiosity. Such is the blessing of time.

To look at Paul's impressive resume, then, is to have a sense of what can be accomplished when we decide to change ourselves and of the new mindset of purpose and meaning that can arise from such deep transformations. The dedication and effort that led Paul to become one of the greatest champions for Christianity of all times could only have come from the singular focus he found in his new purpose. After his encounter with Jesus, Paul developed a clarity of mind peculiar to those who have found their "calling": everything else not germane to their purpose is brushed aside. A "tunnel vision" of purpose takes hold, if you will. Pursuing our purpose brings wholeness, satisfaction and, ultimately, happiness. We have seen this throughout history in our most admirable figures. And that is what we wish for ourselves and those around us.

Let's look at some of Paul's incredible accomplishments to help frame what is possible when we find clarity of purpose and match it to singular focus:

THE APOSTLE OF THE GENTILES

Perhaps Paul's most famous moniker was "the apostle of the Gentiles"—and rightly so. An apostle (from the Greek word *apostolos*) is one who is sent—a messenger, if you will. The "Gentiles," or everyone who is not Jewish, were at the same time the largest group of people in the known world and the group most ignored by early Christians, who also considered themselves Jews. Paul made it his life's work to speak to those who were not Jewish about Christ and his teachings. He was keen to connect and tend to those who were overlooked.

While the early followers of "the Way" were understandably concentrated in Jerusalem and the known Jewish world, Paul followed a different path: he went on to share his knowledge and the new spiritual philosophy with whomever would listen. That included non-Jews. His travels took him beyond Judea and Jerusalem, through Syria, what is today Turkey, Macedonia, Greece, and eventually Italy. All in an era devoid of planes, trains, and automobiles—highlighting his unwavering commitment to his purpose and putting to shame some of today's most prolific frequent flyers.

The job played to his strengths. A well-educated man who spoke many languages and who had a decent amount of travel under his belt already by virtue of having been born in Tarsus (some 350 miles away from Jerusalem by land), Paul was well suited to being the messenger to the Gentiles. More importantly, Paul could speak of his experience: he too had been an outsider to the Christ experience. While recognized as an apostle for the message, he was not one of the 12 original disciples: Paul never met Jesus in the flesh, he never spent time with him, never had a chance to listen to his teachings directly from him, never followed him in his wandering or preachings. Paul was like most of the Gentiles—all who would hear about Christ, but not from Christ. Like us.

Worse (or better) yet, Paul had avidly opposed the new message. As Saul, he had taken on the mantle of defender of the Jewish faith and made a career of chasing down, persecuting, and even executing the followers of what he then perceived to be a new, dangerous cult. Stephen, the first martyr of Christianity, was stoned to death under Saul's auspices after a trial in the powerful Sanhedrin, the Jewish high court of the time. (That is: if the word "trial" can be used for proceedings where prosecutorial and decision-making roles are played by the same party. Anyway, I digress...) Paul's reputation preceded him. It could make the point on its own that at one time Paul had been staunchly opposed to this new Christian philosophy—and then he'd changed. If Christianity's most energetic opponent had yielded to the equitable and hopeful message of Christ's gospel, then certainly this new way of looking at life (and beyond) must be very potent. And divine.

In addition, Paul carried the powerful message that it is not necessary to meet Jesus in person to be transformed by his teachings. Everyone could be changed by the liberating message from this messiah. Physical proximity to the teacher, presence in an ascribed geography, or belonging to a specific group were no longer requirements for spiritual development. Wherever you were, whatever you were, you were qualified to follow Christ. Anyone was good enough to join "the Way," and Paul was the proof. In a way, it was the democratization of Christianity and religious thinking at large.

Also noteworthy is the philosophical shift Paul underwent in his transformation. As Saul he had devoted himself to forcibly preventing his people from straying away from the path he considered right, later as Paul he would focus on inviting people to join him in his new faith. Saul protected, Paul empowered. Saul contained, Paul expanded. Saul persecuted, Paul recruited. Saul monitored, Paul trained. In today's terms: Saul was a compliance officer, and Paul was a visionary leader at a startup.

This change of orientation required work and inner transformation. Paul had to leave behind the comfort of speaking and acting within the Jewish context he knew to explore different contexts he was not as familiar with. Change requires different actions, new habits, a leap from one's comfort zone. In Paul's case, it also required a focus on new people—people whom previously he may have ignored or looked down on. What a change.

Even if it required radical change, Paul must have felt compelled to move forward—because he did, against all odds and, arguably, against "common sense." More, this new message of equity and hope needed to be shared; and it would never spread if Paul had remained within traditional Jewish enclaves. So Paul set forth to travel and take the "good news" wherever he could.[1]

PAUL'S EXTENSIVE TRAVELS

His voyages through the then known world are no doubt impressive—even more so when you consider the times in which they took place. What is most striking, however, is his decision to take them in the first place. The safe approach would be to go spread the word where the word was already known; after all, experts tell us that to grow an existing audience is easier than to create a whole new one. From a personal perspective, it is also a lot more comfortable to remain and act where you are already familiar with. To journey long distances on foot without the benefit of credit cards, cell phones, GPSs, or the certainty of shelter at particular points made travel a much less romantic endeavor than we believe it to be nowadays. Add to it the lack of modern comfortable clothes and shoes, and you remove any aspect of excitement or joy we may believe it to have had. Bluntly put, neither the Food Network nor the History Channel would be interested in a reality show about Paul's day-to-day experiences while on the road. A one-hour special highlighting the destinations? Sure. An in-depth tell-all detailing his daily reality? Unlikely.

Paul traveled great distances, often at great personal risk, because he felt compelled to. Yes, you could argue he did so because remaining in Jerusalem would attract too much attention and opposition from his old colleagues, putting both his life and the nascent philosophy at peril. Yet, he could also have *not* traveled, *not* preached, *not* drawn attention to himself if his main concern was his personal safety. Instead, he could have quietly settled into a comfortable life or taken more time to reflect on what to do, or even decide to disrupt the system from within—all of these were valid options. Options our "common sense" may indeed prefer because they can protect us from hard change. However, Paul pushed forward. He did so despite the challenges ahead because he felt called by his heart to do it. The traveling was not the goal of it for Paul, the sharing of this new message of immortality of the soul was. The benefits and the consolation Jesus's teachings brought people were worth the trouble. Seeing it from that perspective, we can understand why Paul had to go: the message that we never really die (the core of Jesus's teachings) was too good not to be shared with others. That is why Paul traveled.

His travels were incredibly influential. It is in great part due to Paul's traveling that Christian communities in different places took hold. With his mentoring and coaching, they grew and prospered, setting forth a ripple effect that would magnify Christianity beyond the boundaries of Jerusalem. Most of us have heard of these communities: the congregations in Rome; the groups in Corinth, Phillipi, and Thessalonica in modern Greece; and the churches at Galatia, Ephesus, and Colossae in what is today Turkey, to name a few. All of them benefited greatly from his presence and guidance over the years. So much so that they would write to him seeking his advice when he was not present. In a time without email and text messages, members of the nascent churches had to send out messengers with questions to Paul wherever he was. They eagerly awaited his reply to settle internal disputes that challenged their understanding of the new faith and, sometimes, threatened to fracture their budding groups.

All of this paints a picture of a very busy Paul. When he was not on the road traveling, helping establish and grow a new group, or working to sustain himself along the way, he was corresponding with those seeking his wisdom. (Did he even sleep?) All work and no play did not make Paul a dull boy—because for Paul, work was play. That's the only explanation we can find for such a prolific body of work. He was in such demand that he could not be everywhere he was needed. Instead, he did the next best thing: he multitasked and wrote back to those who wanted his help. Some of these writings have lasted to today.

PAUL'S WRITINGS

Writings attributed to Paul have had an oversized influence on the western world. His footprint is all over humanity's bestselling book: the Bible. The "new" half of it, anyway: of the 27 books comprising the New Testament, 13 are attributed to Paul and about half of another, the Acts of the Apostles, deals with his life and works. If you are keeping score, that's almost a perfect half of the basic works of Christianity, the philosophy that has impacted the Western world the most throughout history. After Jesus himself, Paul is the most important exponent of Christianity.

You could argue that not all of the 13 letters attributed to Paul were actually authored by him. You could offer that modern scholars believe that only 7 out of the 13 epistles were penned by Paul—the rest probably written by his followers, maybe even referencing other materials Paul wrote. Or not. Either way, you would probably be right. Regardless, whether Paul is the historical author of all these "deutero-Pauline" letters is beside the point: they were attributed to him because he was important. They were making an argument by authority. Even if all his epistles were counterfeit, forgers elected to lend his name to them because there was no bigger name in early Christianity than Paul's. Since Jesus wisely avoided leaving any writings of his own to us, Paul would be the next man up for anyone trying to lend credence to their thinking. Adding Paul's name to any mix was a sure way to raise eyebrows. Such was the role he played in the spreading of Jesus's teachings early on.[2]

In that manner, historical argumentation aside as to the authorship of all of the letters attributed to him, Paul has cast a long shadow into the world.

It is possible that we might not have Christianity as we do today without his travels and writings. Few documents or artifacts remain of the Christian experience within ancient Hebrew boundaries; most of the books we have in the New Testament, for instance, have been first found (and then translated) from Greek, not Hebrew or Aramaic (Jesus's language). This means that the foundational Christian documents we know today came from the Gentile world—the very world Paul helped seed. Had Paul not been there to lay the groundwork, would these Gentile communities have developed? And if they had not, would we have these key documents? In short, it is hard to imagine a world without

Paul. It is nearly impossible to imagine a Christian world without Paul.

Until Jesus' death, Christianity was the religion of Jesus. After his crucifixion and resurrection, Christianity became a religion *about* Jesus—and much of the "about" came through Paul's perspective. It is his writings that laid the foundation for our modern understanding of Christianity. It is hard to imagine Christianity would be what it is today were it not for Paul. As a matter of fact, it may still have been Judaism.

PAUL'S INFLUENCE

Christianity has become so well known around the world that it is hard for us to conceive that it did not start that way—or that it even risked not being a thing of its own. Let's dive into some numbers to lay the scene for some further considerations.

According to the Pew Research Center, roughly 2.3 billion people called themselves Christians in 2015[3]— about 31% of the world's population. For those of us who like a more concrete measuring stick, about 1 person out of every 3 in the world is Christian. If the world were perfectly mixed (which we can all agree is not), one out of every 3 people you meet or already know would profess a Jesus-based faith. These are substantial numbers. On the other hand, only about 14 million are Jewish, about 0.2% of the world's population. To use our human measuring stick again: if the world were evenly mixed, out of every 1,000 people you met or knew, 2 of them would be Jewish. It's not an exaggeration to say that, when it comes to reach, Christianity has overshadowed Judaism.

We should always beware of arguments by numbers lest we confuse volume with quality. Our point here is not to assert Christianity's superiority over Judaism, but to illustrate that the tail has wagged the dog. Jesus himself was a Jew and, yet, Christianity has become a thing of its own, separate from Judaism. Further, it has grown tremendously over the past two millennia to the point of being the most widespread religious belief system in the world. But how did that happen? How did Christianity come to be something separate from Judaism?

As Christianity began to grow after Jesus's death, a practical question arose amid its Gentile followers: to become Christian, did one need to first convert to Judaism?[4] That's a tough question already in the abstract. It would get even more complex in practical terms. For instance, consider this: should Gentiles wanting to join the early Christian groups first need to be circumcised? No doubt, a sensitive issue for many at the time—and a different level of commitment.

On one side, Jesus was Jewish and even claimed he had come to fulfill the (divine) law and not abolish it. On the other, he departed from established social conventions of the time and would mingle and interact with whoever wanted his company or was in need. In that sense, Jesus was in the unique position of being both a traditionalist and a revolutionary at the same time. While that seemed to work while Christ was around, afterward it became a point of great contention among his followers.

Perhaps to no one's surprise, Paul argued it was not

necessary for Gentiles to first become Jews if they wanted to embrace the teachings of "the Way." In doing so, Paul was indirectly disconnecting Jesus from Judaism. He (and others) probably considered the teachings of Christ to be so deep and broad that they did not necessitate the previous Jewish context to be understood; they could stand alone. He had been interacting with and preaching to the Gentiles already. He knew it could be that way because he was already living it. The issue was likely more of a sticking point for practicing Jews of the time, who probably did not think of it until they started interacting with Gentiles converting to Christianity—and who were then unwittingly led to question their own sense of identity. Were they Jews still or something else? Identity is a tricky thing. Fireworks probably did fly during what we imagine to be some animated discussion amongst early leaders of the nascent philosophy.

Eventually there must have been enough critical mass among them to accept the entry of Gentiles into the new teachings without a prerequisite sojourn into old Jewish customs. Thus, Christianity was decoupled from Judaism and was free to assume a new identity over time. (Grown Gentile men following "the Way"—who sympathized with Paul's position (or vice versa)—probably breathed a sigh of relief.) Paul had done it again: he looked ahead into the future and took a position that would have run contrary to Saul's innermost beliefs.

Paul's courageous stance was less likely a result of a desire to rebel, to stick it to the existing system, than the result of his interpretation of the teachings of Christ. After all, the Christ had been open and accessible to all who would seek him. He had mingled with the poor and the socially unaccepted, with the rich and the privileged alike; he had spoken to Sadducees and Pharisees, and with the Samaritans and the Romans; he even spoke to the so called unclean and to unaccompanied women. It is safe to say Jesus was not into taboos. His approach to teaching revealed an inclination toward diversity, equity, and inclusion—a revolutionary concept even in our days. As such, it would make sense that Jesus's teachings could stand on their own, apart from Judaism. And it remains undeniable that Paul played a key role in that debate and, therefore, in the shaping of the Christianity we know today.

CHRISTIANITY THROUGH PAUL

Paul's accomplishments as an early champion of Christianity are so remarkable that it is sometimes hard to internalize how much influence he has had. In retrospect, other than Jesus himself—who still remains greatly misunderstood to this day—no other person has exerted so much influence on the Western world. Paul's incredible dedication to the living and sharing of this new message of hope led him to traverse vast distances on foot and water to visit a large chunk of the known world then—more than once. Turkey, Greece, even Rome became his backyard. Along the way, he faced unimaginable constraints and challenges that were probably only made less daunting by the fruits of the work he set in motion and saw blossom: new communities of Christians, transforming their own lives through the unparalleled teachings of that prophet from Nazareth.

Paul was the unexpected torchbearer carrying a new message to new people. He took upon himself to leave behind his customs and history to reach out to people different than himself. To do so meant he would be forced to change: he would have to spend time learning new customs and habits as well as finding new ways of communicating with people who did not share his Jewish background. In a way, he was forced to deconstruct his Jewishness, to leave behind that which had made him so successful until then. In time, he became skilled at it: new groups of people, galvanized by his delivery of this new message, grew. And they sought him out for more. So much so they kept asking for his presence and seeking his wisdom even when he was not there with them—such was the impression he left behind.

In the course of trying to attend to the requests of those who wanted more of him and of the new message he carried, Paul wrote. He left us with an impactful written legacy that has shaped thought in the centuries since. Whether we agree on what exactly the legacy is or on its details, its reach nevertheless remains sizable and present —even if it has been manipulated or altered through the times. As we open the New Testament, it is hard not to run into him somehow. As a matter of fact, it is hard not run into Paul everywhere. From landmark architectural feats such as Saint Paul's Cathedral in London to the sprawling megalopolis of São Paulo in Brazil and every-where in between, his name is imprinted on our world in ways that often escape our notice.

The shadow Paul casts in Western history can seem so large at times that makes it hard for us to actually believe the magnitude of his impact. His travels, his writings, his footprint, it all seems supernatural—as if he were just not human. Placing a "Saint" before his name might also make it worse: it subliminally reinforces the idea that Paul may have been a special being, unaffected by the toils and strife to which we are exposed on a daily basis. From that perspective, it can make it harder for us to relate to him and to see how his experiences could relate to ours. Yet, that is not the case. Paul may have been an outlier, but he was certainly human.

SAUL BEFORE PAUL

As we look back into history we often forget that before Paul, there was Saul. Before the torchbearer of new ideas, there was the defender of the old faith; before the coach of new people, there was the monitor of the chosen few; before the humble and selfless martyr, there was the proud and career-driven politician. In short, before "sainthood," there was "humanity." Paul was never perfect, as no human being ever is, but because he ended up his life operating at such a high level one of two things happens in our minds: we either believe him to be supernatural or we deny he existed or did all these things in the first place. The truth is somewhere in the middle: he was a flawed human being, like all of us, who worked so intently on changing that he can be seen as a beacon of light and hope for all of us wishing to change ourselves too. We may not reach Paul-like levels of impact in the world in this lifetime, but we can nevertheless accomplish great things.

That is the message we need to remember: it is

possible to change—and it is worth it to change too. Personal transformation may not happen overnight; it is often a long, arduous process requiring daily effort and commitment. Saul did not become Paul over a matter of hours. It took time. Yet, the fruits of this transformation are real and lasting. In much the same way that we cannot revert Paul's accomplishments and the impact he has had in our world, no one else will be able to undo our own victories either, whenever they come. Simply put, the good we build in this world cannot be ever taken away from us.

We also do well to remember that changing oneself is not about denying who we are or have been. Paul never denied being Saul. He never pretended to be someone else, he just worked hard at being something else. To change, we must also let go of the past; otherwise it takes up too much space in our present—space that's needed for the new, for what's to come. To transform oneself is to open oneself to the different, to the new. If we are holding on to the old, how can we possibly build the new? If Paul had held on to Saul, how could he have become Paul? Changing is also about seizing the moment—every and any moment—, to make the shifts we want to see. It is not about waiting for the right moment to change, but making it. Changing is about choosing. Paul became Paul through hard work, no doubt, but mainly through choice.

Much the same way Paul chose to change and to leave Saul behind on the road to Damascus, we too can choose to change. Whether we are called to change by difficult circumstances or decide to change by our own free will, we would do well to remember change is possible and worthwhile. Saul did it. Change happens all the time around us; people before us have changed and people after us will change. Why not us? We can do it. The question that remains is how. Are there lessons we can learn from others that may ease the process of changing? Something that may offer us some guidance on how to do it? For that, I invite you to follow Paul's footsteps on the road to Damascus so we may learn important lessons from his transformation that we can apply to our own, no matter how big or small they may be.

I will see you somewhere on the road to Damascus.

3
THE STORY

Chances are you have heard it before. Paul's encounter with Jesus on the road to Damascus is a celebrated moment within Christian tradition—and thus a well-known one in the Western world. It is a story that has been repeated millions of times within churches and other places of worship, to the joy of many who have been able to connect with its universal theme of personal transformation and to the dread of others, like churchgoers and Sunday school children everywhere, whose minds were simply elsewhere at that moment. (No judgement here.) Regardless of where you place yourself on that spectrum, and even if you are unfamiliar with some of the details to begin with, it benefits us to quickly review the narrative of Saul's journey to Damascus before we dive in to look at its symbolism.

WHERE IS IT?

The story of Saul's journey to Damascus is found in the Christian Bible. The Bible? You might remember this: the first part, what Christians call the Old Testament, comprises 39 different books and roughly corresponds to what Jews refer to as the Tanakh; the second, the New Testament, consists of 27 books narrating the life and teachings of Jesus and his early followers. Besides being an incredible collection of stories full of great ethical meaning, the Bible also has the honor of being humanity's greatest bestseller, with an estimated 5 billion copies sold.[1] At the same time, it may interestingly hold the status of humanity's least *read* bestseller. (If you have a Bible at home but have never fully read it, you are not alone.)

More specifically, we find the story told over just a few verses in one of the books in the New Testament: Acts of the Apostles. Sometimes referred to as just "Book of Acts" or even just "Acts," the book tells us the history of Christianity in the first century, after Christ's resurrection.[2]

The story of Paul's journey to Damascus (and his so-called "conversion") is mentioned at three different points. In chapter 9, we find a third-person account of the story; in chapter 22, we find Paul's narration of the events in a speech in his own defense while in Jerusalem; and in Acts 26, Paul tells it again, this time to King Agrippa, as part of Roman proceedings. The gist of the story remains unchanged. For your reference, here's the account of Paul's story as seen in the first 19 verses of chapter 9:

Meanwhile, Saul was still breathing out murderous threats against the Lord's disciples. He went to the high priest and asked him for letters to the synagogues in Damascus, so that if he found any there who belonged to the Way, whether men or women, he might take them as prisoners to Jerusalem. As he neared Damascus on his journey, suddenly a light from heaven flashed around him. He fell to the ground and heard a voice say to him, "Saul, Saul, why do you persecute me?" "Who are you, Lord?" Saul asked. "I am Jesus, whom you are persecuting," he replied. "Now get up and go into the city, and you will be told what you must do." The men traveling with Saul stood there speechless; they heard the sound but did not see anyone. Saul got up from the ground, but when he opened his eyes he could see nothing. So they led him by the hand into Damascus. For three days he was blind, and did not eat or drink anything. In Damascus there was a disciple named Ananias. The Lord called to him in a vision, "Ananias!" "Yes, Lord," he answered. The Lord told him, "Go to the house of Judas on Straight Street and ask for a man from Tarsus named Saul, for he is praying. In a vision he has seen a man named Ananias come and place his hands on him to restore his sight." "Lord," Ananias answered, "I have heard many reports about this man and all the harm he has done to your holy people in Jerusalem. And he has come here with authority from the chief priests to arrest all who call on your name." But the Lord said to Ananias, "Go! This man is my chosen instrument to proclaim my name to the Gentiles and their kings and to the people of Israel. I will show him how much he must suffer for my name." Then Ananias went to the house and entered it. Placing his hands on Saul, he said, "Brother Saul, the Lord—Jesus, who appeared to you on the road as you were coming here—has sent me so that you may see again and be filled with the Holy Spirit." Immediately, something like scales fell from Saul's eyes, and he could see again. He got up and was baptized, and after taking some food, he regained his strength.[3]

WHAT IS IT?

The story we find in Acts is a simple one. In it, we find Saul, an influential young Jew making his way to Damascus; he has been authorized by the leader of the Sanhedrin, the highest court in Jewish lands, to seek out, arrest, or kill early Christian preachers. He is going to Damascus on an official mission on behalf of the Jewish faith (read: organized religion).

This is not a weekender or a quick trip: it requires planning and resources. It is an expedition. Roughly 140 miles separate Jerusalem from Damascus "as the crow flies." The modern equivalent would be a trip from San

Diego to Los Angeles, or Rome to Naples, or Berlin to Hanover, or Tokyo to Fukushima, or Sydney to Canberra—but in the windy desert, on foot, and not on modern roads. Without the benefit of planes, trains, or automobiles it was likely close to a two-week trip each way. For that reason, Saul is not alone. There are others with him to help carry the supplies and equipment needed to traverse the distance and feed the team.

Along the way, as the group approaches Damascus, a "great light from heaven"[4] shines on down and causes Saul to fall to the ground. Saul is probably on horseback, which makes the fall even more consequential. It must have been quite a light, quite a dazzling experience to cause Saul to physically lose balance and fall off his mount —especially when you consider Saul was a well-traveled man and was used to horseback riding.

It's not a mere light; Saul has a mystical encounter with something he understands from the start to be out of the norm. A voice then asks: "Saul, Saul, why are you persecuting me?[5]" Saul, trying to make sense of it all, asks for more information. After all, who or what could that be? Clearly this is not your standard everyday experience. The voice reveals itself to be Jesus,[6] whom Saul has persecuted indirectly by chasing his followers.

At this point, we must pause to imagine Saul's surprise and the multitude of thoughts and conjectures running through his mind. After all, much of Saul's energy to date has been dedicated to fighting the spreading of this nascent "cult" and bringing their proponents to "justice." All of a sudden, here he is, face-to-face with Jesus of Nazareth, the very source of his problems.

Taken by the uniqueness of that experience and probably understanding the gravity of the moment in his life,
Saul asks back: "What shall I do, Lord?"[7] The question
itself is loaded with meaning. It reveals the beginning of a
new mindset, a change from his old ways, and a desire to
understand what's ahead. Is this the moment Saul
becomes Paul? The answer he receives, however, is not at
all revealing: Saul is told to go to Damascus and wait.

As the moment fades and the light retracts, Saul is
faced with a new awareness: he can no longer see. He now
finds himself on the road, off his horse, somewhere
between Jerusalem and Damascus, having had an
encounter that is hard to describe or explain—and he is
also blind. The proud Jewish leader now has to be "led by
the hand"[8] by his staff. As if there was not enough on his
mental plate, he now has to navigate life in the first
century without the benefit of sight.

In the middle of it all—after what we can agree is an
unusual experience —Saul has an important decision to
make: does he go back to Jerusalem to regroup and make
sense of what just happened, or does he forge ahead to
Damascus as instructed by the voice of Jesus of Nazareth?
Probably against the suggestion of his travel companions,
who did not experience the event as he did, Saul makes
the courageous decision to proceed to Syria.

Eventually Saul reaches Damascus. He finds shelter (in
what was probably an inn[9]) and waits. "For three days,"
the book of Acts tells us, "he was without sight, and
neither ate nor drank."[10] At this point, it is safe to say,
things are not looking up for Saul—pun somewhat
intended. One of the Jewish world's most powerful

authorities is at an nondescript inn in Damascus, sitting around and waiting for something unspecified to happen, based on the command of the voice of someone he had not previously held in high regard (to put it lightly), received during a mystical experience that took place on a dusty road. He might be thinking, *Maybe all of this was a hallucination. Maybe the unforgivable desert sun and the demanding travel conditions brought all of this about.*

Unbeknownst to Saul, Jesus has also appeared to a man named Ananias, described by the book of Acts as a disciple[11] who was also in Damascus. After what could only have been a very interesting conversation for Ananias —since he knows full well who Saul of Tarsus is and what he has done to followers of the Christ—he agrees to go meet Saul at the inn. There, Ananias lays hands on Saul and tells him he has been sent to heal his sight. "Immediately something like scales fell from Paul's eyes, and he regained his sight."[12]

From there on, things begin to change for Saul. He has reached Damascus as he planned, yet circumstances have changed. Although his initial impetus for traveling to Syria was to find and capture the early proponents of Christianity to bring them back to Jerusalem for punishment, somewhere along the way he began his transformation into one of them. In time, he will acquaint himself with the nascent Christian community of Damascus and, eventually, become the Paul we know in the Western world— one of the greatest communicators of Christianity we have ever had. In the end, the Damascus Saul reached was a very different Damascus than the one he first sought.

AN ASIDE: A STORY BETTER TOLD

If the summary above or the short description found in Acts of the Apostles is somewhat lacking to you or has left you wishing for more, there is an alternative source you may wish to consult. The book *Paul and Stephen* by Francisco Cândido Xavier is a beautiful novel about Paul and Stephen (the first martyr of Christianity, who was killed by Saul's order) that draws readers into the complex web of relationships and circumstances that set the scene for Paul's transformation. Even though Saul's journey to Damascus is a small part of the book, it is certain to enrich your understanding of the subject at hand.

4

THE SEVEN LESSONS BEFORE US

This is where things should begin to get interesting. We have considered why Paul is an interesting model for personal transformation and refamiliarized ourselves with the story. Now our work truly begins.

We now shift our perspective to what Paul's journey can offer us, creatures of the 21st century. Instead of focusing on historical context or his accomplishments as one of the most important voices in the history of the Western world, we will pay attention to the echoes of his footsteps. We leave history somewhat aside to focus on the present and look to the future. We ask ourselves: what can we learn from his experiences? What can we bring into our own lives to help us navigate challenges on the way to finding our own meaning and purpose?

We will consider seven different aspects of his journey and investigate their symbolic meaning and connection to us. Examining these aspects can yield meaningful guidance on how to confront some of the challenges we all face.

The seven lessons we will draw from Paul's journey to Damascus are as follows:

1. IN A GROUP BUT ALONE

Just like Saul on his journey to Damascus, we travel through life in groups. They afford us comfort, protection, and even identity. But none of Paul's colleagues shared his new mindset or joined him in his new life. Personal transformation and spiritual growth are often individual experiences, as they were for Paul. Our timing seldom matches that of those around us. Are we ready to face personal change on our own?

2. A DESTABILIZING MOMENT

The experience that catapulted Paul into great spiritual growth first threw him off his horse. No angels were singing while it happened, and there was no applause. Paul's key moment of change was not pleasant; ours are not likely to be, either. Valuable changes can be hard and come in ways we don't expect. Have we internalized that opportunities for growth do not always come wrapped in a pretty package?

3. THE COURAGEOUS QUESTION

When faced with unexpected adversity, Paul had the presence of mind to recognize his previous approach to life no

longer worked for him. He seized the moment and courageously asked the question, "What would you have me
do?" We too must ask ourselves existential questions on
our way to reinventing ourselves. Are we ready to leave
the past behind?

4. THE TEMPORARY BLINDNESS

After his encounter with Christ, Saul was left blind and
confused for a while. When we are called to change—
either by outside circumstances or by inner conviction—
we too may experience temporary confusion, as our new
end goal may not be readily apparent. We may feel
exposed and vulnerable; we may no longer think we know
what we are about, where we are, or where we should go.
Are we ready to embrace confusion and uncertainty as part
of the journey?

5. THE DECISION TO GO AHEAD

After falling off his horse, having an unexplained vision,
and finding himself blind in the middle of a dusty road,
Paul had an important decision to make: should he retreat
back to Jerusalem or continue his journey to Damascus?
We too will have a choice to make when key opportunities
arise in our lives. Will we retreat into the safety of our old
ways or forge ahead into change?

6. THE UNEXPECTED HELP

Paul is eventually helped by Ananias, who heals him and helps him get started on his new journey. Saul would never have expected to be helped by one of the very people he sought to punish, but Paul was glad it happened. We too will receive help along our journey to change. Will we recognize it and accept it?

7. A DIFFERENT DAMASCUS

The Damascus Saul set out to visit and the one at which Paul arrived were very different from each other—yet they were one and the same. We may end up where we intended to go but see it with very different eyes. This says a lot about how our goals and expectations can change over time. Or how we do. What is your Damascus?

PAUL'S JOURNEY is ripe with symbolic meaning. Some of it we will explore together, some of it you will uncover on your own. Some lessons may appear more relevant than others during specific parts of our lives—all, however, can offer us wisdom in our personal search for our place and purpose in the universe. We could very well have stretched our analysis beyond these seven items as Paul's journey can be seen as an allegory for our lives—but we do not want to overthink things either. Part of the journey is the actual walking, which this book cannot do for you—that is your share. To belabor the journey by remaining in analytical mode for too long would be to do yourself a disservice too. It is time to roll up our sleeves or, if you will, lace up our boots. The road Paul has trodden ahead of us awaits. Shall we follow in his footsteps?

5

LESSON 1: IN A GROUP BUT ALONE

One of the most difficult ideas to take to heart in our journey is that the crucial heavy lifting in our lives must be done by ourselves, individually. It cannot be done by anyone else. We may have a great group of people cheering us on and supporting us along the way, but there comes a time when we must choose for ourselves what we want to do and put in the work to do it. For most of us, it can be a difficult time, and it is not uncommon to feel alone in the struggle. Yet, growth is an individual sport. It takes place within a larger social context, to be sure, but it remains an individual effort. Fortunately, so are its results: because you are the one who did the work, the merit is yours. It is a matter of cause and consequence: you do the learning, you reap the rewards. Still, while we are in the thick of it, we can feel alone in the struggle. That's par for the course or, in our case, par for the road. Paul experienced it—and we are likely to experience it as well. Let's see how.

PAUL'S STORY: IN A GROUP ON THE ROAD, BUT ALONE IN HIS JOURNEY

Saul's trip to Damascus was no small feat. To travel almost 150 miles back then was no small challenge: it required planning, resources, and thick soles—or a sturdy bum, if you had the means to afford horses. Fortunately, Saul had the means. He was traveling for official business. His task: find the early preachers of "the Way" and bring them to justice, whether it be in Damascus or back in Jerusalem.

It would probably take one to two weeks to reach Damascus at that time. You would need the time to prepare and eat your food and find or build shelter every day. If there were any Motel 6 equivalents along the way, it is unlikely they were perfectly spaced to maximize your journey. Thus, there may have been days when you would cover less distance than would be ideal, because it behooved you to sleep in certain places. Moreover, you'd need provisions for yourself, your traveling companions, and your animals, and the extra weight would also slow you down. (You might be able to get them along the way, but would you risk it? Especially if you were accustomed to a certain standard of living, as our young rising star Saul probably was, you probably wouldn't.) For various reasons, the trip would probably take you more than one week.

The trek also required personnel. Someone would have to tend to the animals—and it would not have been Saul. Safety would also be a concern, as much of the way between cities would be sparsely inhabited. If you carried any political power or drew attention to yourself by virtue of your provisions, you would benefit from some sort of security detail. After all, as the old saying goes, there is safety in numbers. It would be no surprise, then, that Saul had a small entourage.

The long hours Saul spent on the road with his fellow travelers—three of them, in Xavier's telling[1]—must have fostered companionship. A six-hour flight across the country may not have (most of) us starting conversation with the stranger seated next to us, but a seven-to-ten-day journey without wifi or in-flight entertainment is an altogether different experience. Much like a long road trip without radio, there is only so much thinking or keeping silent one can do. At some point, there will be conversation. In a ten-day journey, there would be plenty of it.

Saul no doubt developed some sort of relationship with his companions, if he did not know them already. Even though he was the boss, they still walked or rode, ate, and slept as a group. It is possible he may have even picked them for the job for that reason: because he already knew them. (If you had a choice, would you not prefer to travel with people with whom you are comfortable?) Even if Saul did not know them, which doesn't seem to be the case, by mid-journey he would have. There would have been plenty of time, and even casual conversation has a way of revealing who we are and what we are about. Also, remember: they were each other's security. Given their stations in life, they may not have shared a deep personal friendship as equals, but there almost certainly was a sense of companionship and partnership during the trip.

So when Saul fell off his horse and shared he was blind, they would have genuinely cared. When he described his experience of having heard the voice of Jesus of Nazareth, the prophet who was crucified and killed, they would have been truly worried for Saul. They would have exchanged puzzled looks amongst themselves not just because he was their boss, but because they knew Saul's character and that the purpose of his trip was to chase the followers of the very man he purported to just have met in a mystical experience. That would not have been characteristic of Saul at all. They would have discussed, maybe even in front of Saul, what to do next. To hear the most aggressive persecutor of Christianity say he has changed his mind, all of a sudden, would be surprising. To find he would now follow the directions he received in a vision from a dead prophet to go to Damascus, would be even more perplexing. They cared for him, but certainly the desert sun must have got to Saul. Surely many travelers before them had fallen victim to the desert. Long days on the road without adequate shade, poor hydration, not enough rest, and maybe a faster pace so they could make it to Damascus quicker. All of these could contribute to any traveler falling off his horse and hallucinating. One can see how Saul's companions could have entertained these thoughts: they would not be out of the realm of possibility. In fact, they were more probable and rational than the explanation he actually gave.

One can also imagine the weight of that moment for Saul's companions. Here they were, in the middle of the road, faced with their boss and friend saying things to them that were uncharacteristic of the Saul they knew. That is after he has fallen off his horse without provocation. And he was now blind. What should they do? Saul insisted they should continue to Damascus, but maybe the prudent thing would be to return to Jerusalem so he could receive proper care. In Jerusalem, they would have more resources; Saul's friends, family, and even the Sanhedrin would know what to do. What if something worse happened to Saul on their way to Damascus? Would they be held responsible for it? He was important; there were a lot of things to consider. Saul wanted to go forward. He was technically their boss, but should they listen to him? Should you listen to someone who is not well about matters of their own health? And if not, how would they convince Saul to go back? They certainly would have tried. Could they force him to return? Should they wait a while to see if he would improve? We have no way of knowing how long the situation might have taken, but no doubt it must have been a delicate moment for Saul's traveling companions. In Xavier's historical novel, a compromise is reached: two members of the group return to Jerusalem to let the Sanhedrin know what has happened to one of its most promising young members, and one proceeds to Damascus with Saul.[2] After all, it would have been nearly impossible to bend Saul's will.

By the time Ananias healed Saul's blindness in an inn on "the street called Straight,"[3] there are no more mentions of Saul's companions. They have all left him. Maybe he has sent the final companion back, but either way he is alone. The fact that Saul is at an inn is itself a telling detail. As a prominent political figure, Saul would have been extremely well connected. As the custom of the time would have it, he would typically have been hosted at the home of a political official or influential friend. Under normal circumstances, the honor of hosting Saul would have been coveted, a sign of status. Inns, where a traveler who knew no one in the region would stay, would have been the last resort for someone like Saul.

It's likely that Saul was politely turned away by his influential friends. As Saul told them his story and shared his mystical encounter and his new respect for the resurrected prophet from Nazareth, his connections made the political calculation that it would be a liability to host him. Saul was suddenly and radically rebelling against the status quo of which he had been the embodiment just a couple of days before. To be associated with his new views, with this new Saul, would be tantamount to political suicide for those who were comfortable with the world as it was. Had they thought he was unwell, they would have cared for him—but he was not. He was coherent, could talk and express himself well. He had just changed, and their worldviews no longer aligned. So his so-called friends avoided him. Saul was on his own from then on—figuratively and literally.

Let's imagine what was going through Paul's head:

Blind, alone, unkempt, and probably low on resources, Saul could only wait at the modest room in the inn at straight street hoping he had made the right choice. He knew not what lay ahead of him, but his heart had told him to follow the voice only he had heard—and so he did. Doubt and long hours of second-guessing must have kept Saul company during those days he lay in wait. His mind racing, he probably wondered: had he done the right thing? Should he go back? He probably could; he could write it all off as the sun and the harshness of the desert. He could have it all again: the comfort, the acceptance, the fame. His old life must have beck-

oned, but his heart had changed. *Something deep inside told him he had to change even though the whole world seemed to point the other way. So he waited. Eventually, Ananias showed up unexpectedly to his room at the modest inn and, from there, Saul found a new way forward. And the rest is history.*

OUR LESSONS: A HARD REALIZATION

The first lesson we can take from Paul's journey to Damascus is that we, too, may feel alone during important times in our lives. No matter how sociable and well-connected we are, we will go through moments when we must make key decisions no one else can make for us. These moments are always difficult and emotionally taxing.

It is also very likely that the people to whom we feel closest may not be always present—emotionally or otherwise. Perhaps our most trusted advisors passed away before those moments of great decision. Perhaps they are still with us but don't understand our choices, our motivations. In some cases, they may decide not to support us during important moments of our transformation, and may even choose to stop associating with us.

This can be hard to stomach, but it's not a reflection on who you are. It's a reflection of who *they* are—or, rather, where they are in their own journeys. Without judgment, we must understand that people take different paths at different times, and they may or may not coincide with ours. That's OK—and you will be OK, too. We are all on our road to Damascus—just not at the same time and not in the same place. When we become aware of this, when we understand the process, it makes it easier to bear it. When we know what is coming, it helps us prepare for the road ahead. It may not necessarily remove all the pain and frustration of going through these difficult moments, but it may lessen them. What is important is to remind ourselves that this is but a step in our road to change—and that this phase will pass too, like it did for Paul.

DIFFERENT PEOPLE AT DIFFERENT TIMES

Paul had different people exit his journey at different times. In Xavier's telling of Paul's story, two of his companions turned back to Jerusalem while he was still on the road and the third returned home when they reached the inn; other former allies probably turned away from him in Damascus.[4] Ultimately, Paul had to stand alone.

Symbolically, we can take those who were on the road with him as our closest relationships. These are the people with whom we spend the most time and share most of our experiences. Perhaps they are our family members whom we live with, the partners we choose for ourselves, or even our work colleagues whom we see every day. In many different ways, they may have worked, eaten, and slept by our side. Yet, as much as we enjoy their company, there is no certainty that they will reach the end of our journeys with us. Is that even a fair expectation of those in our inner circle? Probably not. Some of our support system will leave us through physical death; some others because of varying circumstances; and others still will be with us almost to the end of our journey before they go on their way and leave us to make our own decisions—much like Paul's three companions.

Then there are less intimate but still important relationships—with family members with whom we do not interact as often, good old friends we have not spoken to in a while, or more distant colleagues. We may not expect as much from them as of our closer companions, but nevertheless we count on their support. They, too, may not come through as we wish or expect. We need to be emotionally prepared for that as well.

An important aside: we are focusing on loss and solitude here, but *not everything needs to be doom and gloom*. It is very important to also say we are not fated to just losing people along the way. We shouldn't roll up in a defensive crouch and eschew human interaction because people will eventually leave us. That is not the point at all. We are going to gain companions on the road and receive unexpected help too. This will not be our permanent reality— just the first step of our journey of self-awareness and enlightenment. That was not what defined Paul, after all. So hang on while we make our way through it. With that in mind, we continue our exploration...

LOSING PEOPLE

We have few certainties from the moment we are born into this world. Benjamin Franklin wisely posited that death and taxes were two of them. Another is that we will lose people along the way. Whether due to age or circumstance, the end of our journey will see us surrounded by a different group of people than those with whom we started it. As travelers, we need to be aware and ready for that.

Let us take the varnish of emotion off for a second and look at things objectively. We know our first companions, our parents, are likely to leave us by reaching the end of their current journey on earth before we do. We also know our children, if we have them, will also eventually leave the nest to embark on their own journey. Our friends may move away when life calls them to new adventures. Our life partners, perhaps, are more likely to stay with us for our entire lives—but that is not guaranteed either.

The undeniable gist of it is that we will lose travel companions while we are on the road. We may not lose all of them, like Paul seemingly did while on his journey, but lose some we will. There are no "if"s and "but"s about it—only "when"s and "how"s.

Rather than fight the impossible battle not to lose anyone while on the road to Damascus, our energy may be best spent in preparing for the inevitable: we will lose travel companions along the way. After all, there is no point in fighting absolute certainties. It is best to prepare to move through them.

The question then becomes: how do we handle loss? How do we best prepare for what is to come? The how may be more important here: if we understand how we may lose people along the way, we may be better able to handle it when it happens. So let us turn our attention for a few moments to preparing ourselves; let us spend some time thinking about how we may lose people and how we can react to such loss.

At the risk of oversimplifying things, we lose people on

our road to Damascus for one of two reasons: physical death or a change in circumstances. Both are hard because dealing with loss is always hard. Both have their own idiosyncrasies, and that is why we are separating them. Some people find one kind harder than the other, but this is no pain Olympics: it is not about figuring out which hurts the most, but preparing ourselves to navigate the situations ahead of us. We must always beware of getting trapped in "pain Olympics mode," because when we compete with others to see who is hurting the most, we trap ourselves in the pain we want to escape from and begin to assume it as part of our identity. When pain becomes part of our identity, of whom we think we are, it is even harder to move away from it. So, let's step away from this pernicious pitfall and remind ourselves that pain is only a temporary condition. Regardless of which type of loss may be harder for you, you can still benefit from getting ready, from adopting a new mental perspective. In the following sections we will explore both scenarios and how we can best prepare to face them.

LOSING PEOPLE: PHYSICALLY

Wait a minute... How did this all of a sudden move into "d"-word territory? Are we really going to talk about death here? Yes! While there is no physical death in the story of Paul's journey on the road to Damascus, the narrative is ripe with symbolic deaths: deaths of relationships and even identities. Physical death is inevitable—and something we would do well to ponder more frequently. For our purposes, death also comes into play.

Whether it is by natural causes which come at a ripe old age or through an unforeseen circumstance, there is no denying Benjamin Franklin was right: death is a certainty. When we read his maxim, we often think of our own deaths, but we should also turn our attention to the possibility that it may first find those around us. It is also not uncommon for fellow travelers to report their journey is made harder by the absence of someone important to them who passed over. Perhaps it was the supportive mother or father who was always at the ready to dispense wisdom in the toughest of moments, the accepting friend who was keen to listen to our challenges in a nonjudgmental way, or the life partner who was ever ready to encourage us not to give up. You name it: the cases are as varied as the relationships we used to have—and for which we now long. The passing of time may sometimes help lessen the vacuum they seem to have left in our lives, but it will never take away the fact we had them with us for a while and now we no longer do. Nor should it.

But it does not always have to be painful and grim: instead of focusing on the hole we sometimes think their passing has left in our lives, maybe we can instead hone in on what we have gained because of them. What have they added to our lives? What have we learned because of them? What is it that we did not have before we met them but now do? What was their gift to us?

It is as much about what you can take away as it is about what they have left behind. The mark of excellent relationships is the coexistence of both: the perpetual legacy of the give-and-take that happens between two parties. Naturally, we are talking about the emotional, intellectual, or spiritual take-aways and leave-behinds—not the physical. As Siddhartha Gautama, the Buddha, told us 2,500 years ago: all suffering and strife come from attachment to impermanent things. If we remain focused on the physical, we are bound to suffer, as physical things are impermanent by nature. They simply cannot and do not last. All that we see around us will eventually falter and decay—bodies included. Not even the most skilled plastic surgeons and doctors can deter the inevitable progress of time—try as they might and as much as we want them to.

On the other hand, if we focus on lasting things, the story can be different. We can turn pain and grief into gratitude. Multiple great sages agree: Jesus complements the teaching of Buddha by suggesting where we should place our attention instead: "lay up for yourselves treasures in heaven, where neither moth nor rust destroys and where thieves do not break in and steal."[5] Their philosophy is psychologically powerful. That is to say: if we focus on the intangible treasures we have gained through and because of our relationships, if we remember the true essence of those who no longer are with us and their legacy, we will never lose them—they can never be taken away from us. They will be with us permanently, whether you believe in an afterlife or not. The value they add to our lives is simply undeniable.

The fundamental question we must answer for ourselves when it comes to the so-called "loss" of people is if we are going to stand in the deficit camp or on the abundance team. Will we think the glass is half empty because those we care for are no longer with us or will we see it as half full because we carry forth our shared experiences and the learning they made possible for us? Will we choose to look upon our memories with sadness or honor the relationships we forged and value them through gratitude? We may waver but, ultimately, we need to pick sides.

It may strengthen our resolve to shift viewpoints and imagine the situation not from our perspective, but theirs: how would they want us to remember our relationship? Would they want it to be something that holds us back and drags us down, or would they prefer it to be a gift that helps us move forward? If the relationship was healthy, it will certainly be the latter. At the risk of beating a dead horse, if the roles were reversed, wouldn't you wish that they too could look back on your relationship in a way that helps them move forward?

Ultimately, it is up to us whether we will "lose" those who have passed on or take them with us on our journey. We lose them by thinking they are no longer with us; we carry them on the road with us by treasuring our time together and the lessons we learned. Put another way: have they really left us? Independent of our beliefs in an afterlife, it is our choice to determine how we will see it. Shifting mindsets is an arduous thing, especially in a society that often expects us to value the departed through sadness instead of gratitude. Fortunately, we are in control of how we live our lives—it is our decision. It only takes our will and effort to make it happen.

In a roundabout way, we reach an important realization: those who leave this earth while we are on our journey do not really leave us. They just become invisible to the eye—but remain tangible in our feelings and memories, a brick in the edifice of our ongoing self-creation cemented by the common experiences and learning we have shared.[6]

If we accept that to be the case, it may be even easier to process loss through death than through other circumstances.

LOSING PEOPLE: EMOTIONALLY

Another challenge we will certainly face in our lifetimes is the loss of people, emotionally speaking. Such losses happen when we think we no longer have those we value or esteem by our side during important moments of our lives.

If and when we are called to change, confusion generally ensues. Like Saul's travel companions, yours might experience confusion or doubt. Perhaps they may think your new choices and motivation are a sign that you are not well. Perhaps they figure you have been working too hard and just need some time to recover. Perhaps they will have other explanations. Whatever angle they are coming from, it is important to remember some people you are close to will struggle to understand why someone they knew well decided to do something different. Their level of confusion will likely vary according to the degree of change you are embarking on and how much of a departure that is from their own values and experiences. If the change you seek is something they have gone through or understand, they are more likely to support you; if it is outside their realm of experience, they may struggle to understand it—and thus support you through it.

At the end of the day, there is no specific rule as how people will react to you changing. Because they are different individuals with different backgrounds and experiences, each may react differently. Only those closest to them will be able to better assess how they will respond—and you are one of them! So it will be incumbent on you to try to understand where they are coming from, where they are at, and where they will likely go. This is probably not what most of us want to hear when we are struggling through a change process: that we may need to stop and think about the people we wish were thinking about us. Nevertheless, if we want to communicate well with them, if we want their support, if we want to understand how they see our change, this might be the best way to go. To be understood, we must first seek to understand. We need to step out of our moment and try to see it through their eyes.

The good news is that you do not need to know a person's life in full to be able to do it. There are certain general thoughts and considerations we can entertain that may help us with everyone we meet, even if they are all different.

RELATIONSHIPS

We meet thousands of people over the course of our lifetimes: our family, our friends, acquaintances, schoolmates, work colleagues, affinity groups—so many people it is hard to precise a specific number. The number is so large it is nearly impossible to remember them all. Naturally, our relationships are at different levels; we have not developed deep connections with all of them. Relationships require common experiences, and common experiences require time—and we just do not have enough time in one lifetime to develop meaningful relationships with everyone we meet. Still, they are all important and should be acknowledged in different ways.

Nevertheless, the more time we spend with people, the more likely we are to care about their opinion and acceptance—and even expect their understanding and support. Of course, there are exceptions, like those people you meet along the way and it quickly feels like you have known them forever. Perhaps we have but, by and large, the thought holds true: the more time we spend with people, the deeper our connection. When support and acceptance from those closest to us is absent, that is when it hurts the most. That pain can be seen as a testament to the value we place on our relationships—and on the time and common experiences we have shared.

When we are able to see relationships as a factor of time and shared experiences, we can challenge our belief that people are fixed quantities. When we do so, it makes it easier for us to afford them more grace. People are always growing, transforming, changing—just as we are. We know this because, at one point before in our history, the relationship did not yet exist. Then we met, spent time together, and that changed: a relationship developed. The time we spent sharing experiences together, interacting, and influencing each other is what built the relationships we now share. That they may not be able to support us during a specific moment of your life does not mean they will never be able to support us again. They too can change. Nor does it mean that they do not care for us, or that their support at other times was false.

Interestingly, however, when we find ourselves in a situation where the people we expected to understand and support us do not do so, we often assign painful narratives to the situation. We think that since they are not behind us now, they will never support us again, or that they no longer care for us, or that in fact they never cared for us to begin with. None of these are necessarily true—they are just emotional defense mechanisms we use to protect ourselves when we think people are fixed quantities. We vilify them to make it easier for us to write them off -- lest we continue to hurt.

With a broader perspective, these defense mechanisms are no longer necessary: when we remember that our family, friends, and colleagues are fluid and changing—just like we are—we can become more accepting. Making the shift to understanding people as multidimensional beings helps us weather the challenge of not always receiving the acceptance, understanding, or support we would like from them.

It might just be a matter of timing: that our change is happening on a schedule that does not necessarily match theirs, that we are at different places on the road to Damascus. They may not be in sync with your desires and path right now but, works in progress that they are, they may be later. It is not necessarily the end of the relationship—just a hiatus of affinity.

Do you want to be pessimistic for a second? The most

pessimistic approach we can take is to think that we may never again see eye-to-eye—but that does not negate that we have seen eye-to-eye (or heart-to-heart) before. If they are not heading the same way we are, we can still be grateful for having had a chance to walk together for part of the road. We can still wish our paths will cross again, and they may—especially when the only constant we have is change.

Moreover, it is our choice as to which lens we use to see the world. Why not simply harbor the idea they can change too, like we do? If we are seeking their support while we are transforming ourselves, why would we think they cannot change and transform themselves too? In a way, everything is always in transition.

As we recenter our worldview around the idea that all people (ourselves included) are fluid and constantly changing, it helps us depersonalize our negative interactions. Our loved ones are, like us, constellations of experiences, worries, and ideas and may be struggling with their own problems invisible to us. In doing so, we become more accepting and tolerant of others, just like we would like them to be of us. It is a corollary of the golden rule, if you will.

When we internalize that people are always changing and that their behaviors are a response to their trying to be happy on their own road to Damascus, we let go of the emotional charge we often build up when we feel those we care about are absent from or not supportive at the important moments or milestones in our lives. They are not doing it deliberately against us or to spite us; they simply cannot see why we would make such choices or are unaware of how important these choices may be for us because it may not feel the same to them. As we tear down these self-centered stories we create in our minds and substitute them for what they really are—humans trying to lead their lives the best way they know how —we release a great emotional charge we created for ourselves. We worry less about our own worth and about what we have done wrong; we focus less on the frustration of not having them present; we harbor less negative thoughts in general; and we may even feel better physically, as all of this worry and negative focus takes a toll in our physical bodies as well.

In short, there are many upsides to being more tolerant of others through seeing them as multifaceted beings, including freeing ourselves to focus on what we want to do anyway: move ahead on the road of change. Letting go of our own unhelpful thoughts and of what holds us back is a gift we could give ourselves more often. After all, true change begins with us—not others.

GAINING PEOPLE

While we are on the road, we have only so much time and space. We often focus so much on trying not to lose things or on dragging people we have known down our path with us (whether they like it or not) that we forget the road ahead is better than the one behind us—because the road ahead of us is that of personal growth. The same applies to people in our lives. In the midst of all our worries, while we are afraid of losing people we like, we fail to remind ourselves that we will meet new travelers on the road—and that in time, they too may become great friends, great relationships. It is hard to let go of what we have without first seeing what we may gain, but it is exactly being open to what is ahead that allows us to add to our roll of relationships. We all probably prefer certainty: we would all like to know what we are gaining before we have let go of anything. But growth is not about letting go of the old after we have the new; it is about letting go of the old to make space for the new. Life is not about certainty, but discovery.

Building new relationships seems to get harder as we get older. Why is that? Is it because we lose our openness to the world? Is it because we are afraid of exposing ourselves to others and invite them into our intimacy? Whatever the source of the problem, the solution remains the same: we just have to put ourselves out there and try to meet new people, to make new friends, to build new relationships.

Children often seem to be perfectly capable of striking up conversations with other children at parks, sport events, restaurants—everywhere, really. And if children can, why can't we? We absolutely can if we remove the patina of social conventions and fear of rejection we have accumulated over time. When we consider that rejection is not an indication of the worth of the person reaching out but that the other person is unwilling to engage, being open to others becomes easier. The "other" may choose not to engage for a variety of reasons, including their own fear of rejection. We are often so trapped within our own sense of inadequacy that we fail to consider that the "other" may be as hesitant to engage as we are, if not more so; that they too worry we will eventually refuse them. And so we ensnare ourselves in this social trap, in which we do not reach out to others because we are afraid they may refuse us, and they do not reach out to us because they worry we will reject them. This silent dance is made worse and even slower when we feel we already have a support system in place. If we think we already have enough friends, we can rationalize not trying to make new acquaintances and build new relationships. Thus, we watch more and more Netflix and YouTube and work longer and longer hours to occupy our time.

However, no one is an island, entirely by themselves, as the poet John Donne would rightly remind us. We crave human connection as we are social beings by nature. When our emotional support systems are lacking, we struggle. As a result, we are almost always compelled to seek human connection to shore up the foundations of our emotional well-being and fill the vacuum left by those who previously occupied that space. That we seem to instinctively know.

What we sometimes forget is that, while there are people occupying the space, we may not feel like we really need to open ourselves to new relationships. Losing some of our travel companions along the way forces us to do that which we did not before: open ourselves up to having new people come into our lives. It happened to Paul: he was open to being healed by Ananias because he had parted ways with other people. Healing may not have happened for him if all his travel companions were also in the room with Ananias.

With new people come new experiences and new

learning. When we think of it more deeply, that appears to be exactly the kind of thing we need when we are trying to change ourselves or our lives. Since we may need a push to be open to making new connections, losing people is sometimes a good nudge toward the very change we seek.

The universe has a funny way of pushing us forward at times. Much of it deals with a change in mindset: our own mindset. Thus we find ourselves faced with an important choice: we can put our energy toward trying to hang on to our relations who may be drifting away from us, or we can channel it into building new ones. We can try to hold on to the status quo or embrace change.

To be clear: we are not talking about a fire sale here, with an "everyone must go" mentality. It is not about jettisoning all your existing relationships for the sake of changing. It is not others that change us; it is we that change ourselves in interacting with others. What we are proposing is opening oneself to new relationships and reminding ourselves that we will meet great people on our road to Damascus. Paul himself came upon a whole new set of relations after his journey to Damascus. He traveled the known world building new relationships—and in that he was extremely happy. By looking forward, he created a new reality. So let us remind ourselves that this too can happen to us: although we may lose some along the way, we are bound to meet others. It is the in-between that feels the hardest, but that is only temporary.

ALONE DOES NOT MEAN LONELY

It is not uncommon for us to feel lonely at key points in our lives. Paul, no doubt, felt very lonely as he waited alone at the inn in Damascus for what was next for him. Blind and by himself, with his life upended by an unexpected event and his future unclear, he was both alone and lonely. Yet it bears mentioning that there is a big difference between being alone and feeling lonely. Being alone is having no one else present. Being lonely is feeling solitary or sad because one does not have friends or company. You can be alone but be thoroughly enjoying yourself. Take, for instance, reading a good book, basking in a beautiful view, revisiting great memories, enjoying good music, meditating, exercising, and so on. All of these can be done when we are by ourselves and all and can be very pleasant. We can also be surrounded by people and yet feel very lonely; we have all been to a party or two where we did not know anyone, felt that we had nothing in common with people in a group, or spent time with people with whom we felt we could not show our true selves.

The truth is that we can feel lonely in a crowd and happy alone. Having people around us is not necessarily a recipe for happiness. Having the right people around us, however, can be a catalyst to happiness. Happiness remains an individual sport: it is not an external commodity but an internal mindset. It cannot be gifted or purchased: it has to be built within.

That is not to say we need to be alone to be happy or that we cannot be happy in a group: we need to learn to do both. We can be happy whether we are alone or in a group. To do that, we need to be more OK with ourselves. When we are in balance with ourselves, when we accept who we are or want to be, we crave acceptance less. In that moment we stop being lonely.

Of course, we may have moments of loneliness; moments during which we lapse into forgetting who we are or who we want to be. That is only normal—and human. Yet, we now know better: we know these moments are temporary stages and that being alone does not mean we have to feel lonely. We can give ourselves permission to feel lonely for a little while if we wish. After all, we cannot control our emotions, and it is important to acknowledge and process them. But we should beware of dwelling in that space for too long lest it becomes a self-imposed reality. We should resist letting it become a "pity party" of one as it can quickly devolve into depressive states that do not do us any favors. Imagine what would have happened if Saul had given up due to loneliness and fear when he was waiting, uncertain, in the inn. If he had returned to Jerusalem, or descended into the absolute depths of despair, sure that his situation would never improve, and perhaps taken his own life. He would not have had the deeply meaningful experiences that defined his life, and we all would have lost the contributions he made after going on to become the Paul we know. The world would be a very different place. The same applies to us: whether we think so or not, whether we are aware of it or not, we all have too much to offer to the world to let loneliness paralyze us.

So we should actively remove the burden from ourselves of thinking that whenever we are alone we should feel lonely, and whenever we are lonely we'll be lonely forever. Being alone on the road is temporary and transitory. Just as we use our time with others to interact, exchange ideas, and receive feedback, we can leverage "alone time" to reflect, to plan, to rest even. Both can help inform what can come or what we want to come next while we are on the road.

WHAT WE LEARN FROM PAUL AND THE ROAD

The first lesson we can learn from Paul's journey to Damascus is that we are ultimately responsible for our choices. This incredible responsibility is at the same time hard and nontransferable. When key moments for change present themselves to us, they can be made even more emotionally taxing and demanding as we realize we must tackle them by ourselves. In that, we may feel alone even if we have a strong support system or a large social circle.

As Paul found himself accompanied by others on the road to Damascus, so do we during our lifetimes. His mystical encounter with Christ, however, was an individual event—as was his decision to pursue the path toward change. He found himself on a separate trajectory, no longer accompanied by the same companions. So too will be the key growth experiences in our lives: we cannot expect that those around us will necessarily be part of them, much less understand them, even if they have walked a long distance by our side. We must therefore be prepared to lose people along our journey—and be OK with it. Whether we lose them to death of the physical body or to emotional unavailability, we must make peace with the fact that their leaving us is not a reflection of our worth but a simple inevitability. They are on their own journeys. Sometimes our paths cross for short periods of time, sometimes for longer ones. Regardless, we will always have the memories and benefit from the time we spent together during our treks—and it behooves us to focus on what we have gained rather than mourning what we have lost. When we do so, they never really leave us.

We are also reminded that change requires changing— not of others, but of ourselves. By definition, we cannot change by remaining the same—so we must learn to let go of the expectation that our fellow travelers should or will follow us on our new path. (After all, we cannot control what others do or do not do. In fact, we can barely control ourselves at times...) As we free ourselves from this self-centered perspective, we make space for the new, for what is to come, and for our old friends to fully be themselves, just as we want to be. At the same time, we make space for new relationships that are bound to come in time. Because just as we will certainly lose people while on our journey, we will also gain new ones. It happened to Paul; it will happen to us—because it has always happened to us and to the world ever since we were children. We have constantly built new relationships in our lives and survived it all. We may be a little rusty, but we have done it before.

Paul's journey to Damascus also leads us to reflect on solitude—and whether we make the proper distinction between feeling lonely and being alone. Without a doubt, there will be countless moments in our lives when we will be alone—the challenge, however, will be to minimize the times where we will feel lonely. That is perhaps the greatest challenge of our times: to understand that solitude is a temporary stage, a phase that calls and allows for inner reflection ahead of great and beautiful growth that lies ahead. These difficult lonely moments are when we make space for new and greater things to come. Saul was forged into Paul by the searing heat of difficult times when he felt lonely and the hammering of the convictions that told him he must go ahead into uncharted territory because his encounter with the Christ was beyond anything else he had known to date. Ultimately, this painful process on the anvil of life yielded beautiful results in a new and resplendent Paul who became a tool for greater good and changed the world. We too are fated to success of differing degrees.

What remains ahead for us on our road to Damascus may not always be clear. But in Paul's experiences we have a blueprint for the process through which personal change occurs. When we know the process and the steps along the way, our anxiety can be mitigated, our challenges better understood, and certainty can be gained about the next steps we will face in our personal journey toward individual growth. In that, confusion and suffering can be made less because the path becomes more predictable. And when we have a better picture of what is down the road for all of us, we can better prepare to navigate it. In that manner, we now are better equipped to be alone during the most challenging moments of our lives even if we are in a group—and be OK with it.

6

LESSON 2: A DESTABILIZING MOMENT

O ur second stop on the road to Damascus is the actual moment when Saul meets the Christ. In fact, it is fair to say it is less of a meeting and more of a fall. And an important fall it is: it is about those moments where life throws us a curveball—one which sometimes hits us right in between the eyes and knocks us to the ground. It is about those moments that destabilize us and send us reeling. It is about the lessons we learn when we fall off our horse, much the same way Paul fell off his. In essence, the second lesson we learn on the road is about those tough moments in our lives where things take a turn for the unexpected—and how we can react to it.

In retrospect, years later we often find ourselves grateful for these moments because they pushed us forward—but that is hard to recognize when we are in the heat of things. Painful moments are important moments. They bring the awareness that big changes in our lives can often start with difficult situations. It is the breaking of idealistic expectations we sometimes inexplicably hold in our minds that change and progress will always come through a gentle and pleasant process, bringing us only joy along the way. Yet, the opposite is often true. In facing the unexpected, the painful, the shocking, we realize we must or want to change. Consider them life's very own wake-up call service. That is how it happened to Paul—and how it may also happen to us.

This should come as no surprise. We see this everyday —whether it be in the challenges others around us are facing or because we are living it ourselves. Perhaps it is the end of a marriage or long partnership in ways we did not want or see coming, and which makes us feel betrayed or untethered. Maybe it is the loss of a loved one so dear to us that we do not know how to fill the vacuum left in our lives. It could be a move to a new place with habits, customs, or language different from the ones to which we are accustomed, leaving us feeling disconnected and lonely. We might lose a job or a career we cared deeply about or really needed to financially sustain us. An illness could substantially change our ability to move about or perform how we once did. Whatever form it may take, we see it around us every day: moments that destabilize us, challenges that knock us to the ground.

The natural question that follows, then, is what does Paul's journey to Damascus have to teach us? What can we learn from Paul's experience about such moments? Let us return to our story...

PAUL'S STORY: A DESTABILIZING MEETING WITH THE CHRIST

They have been on the road for a while. Saul and his companions move forward to Damascus like all other travelers would: slowly and steadily. As the caravan inches ahead, the desert sun falls heavy on their backs, and the horse under Saul feels warm. Barring the occasional settlement along the way, the landscape does not change much. As they continue their solitary march, the dusty road seems to do two things at once: to go on forever and to emanate the reflected heat of a Mediterranean sun unconcerned with the welfare of travelers. Days on the road have exhausted much of the conversation. As they approach Damascus, the atmosphere is one of reflection and silence brought about by the long journey. Our traveling party moves forward.

All of a sudden and to everyone's surprise, Saul falls from his horse onto the road. As Acts describes it, a "great light from heaven"[1] shines down and causes Saul's fall. What follows for Saul is an indescribable experience of meeting with Christ and feeling something until then unbeknownst to him.

What matters most for us, however, is that in one brief moment Saul's entire life is upended by that encounter. After that, everything changes for him. The man who emerges from the experience is different: that moment gives birth to Paul. And if we think about it, all of that happens on the ground—on the dusty and unkempt surface of a road to Damascus. It is on the ground—surprised and probably in pain—that Saul has his transformative encounter with Christ. The rest, as we say, is history.

OUR LESSONS: DEALING WITH THE UNEXPECTED

If you think the wrenches the universe throws at you sometimes seem odd, consider Paul: what must have been the most consequential moment of his long life was one he did not expect. One no one could really expect. Saul could never have imagined that, on his way to hunting down another early Christian, he would have run into the apparition of the very prophet who started the movement he sought to end—a dead prophet, mind you —and that because of this encounter he would substantially change his worldview and purpose. Can we all agree this is not the sort of thing we plan for in the morning before we go about our days? Can we also settle on the fact this is not something you can really prepare for?

Yet this became Paul's reality. Luckily for us, his story can serve as a blueprint to what we can expect when we face extremely hard moments in our lives. We may not literally fall off a horse in a dusty road somewhere between Jerusalem and Damascus, but we will all face adversity in our lives. We are all facing or will face an internal battle no one else can perfectly understand. The questions we want answers for are: how can we handle it? What can we do to stop the pain and get ourselves back into a position where we feel we have control and agency over our lives? Fortunately, the road to Damascus is ripe with rich symbolism we can untangle together and put to use in preparing ourselves for the unexpected. For our purposes, we will focus on three symbolic aspects of Saul's experience in this chapter: the light, the fall, and the ground.

A LIGHT THAT KNOCKS US DOWN

It must have been quite a light to cause Saul to physically lose balance and fall off his horse—especially when you consider Saul was a well-traveled man who was used to riding on horseback. When was the last time you were knocked down by light? Alright, let's not be coy about it: it must have been more than a light, otherwise we would have millions of accidents throughout the world as people flip their light switches on for various purposes everyday. Imagine: our nightstand lamps would knock us out, flashlights would become Jedi lightsabers, and car headlights weapons of mass destruction... Light humor apart (pun intended), we are clearly not talking about everyday light here. What light was it, then, that knocked Saul off his horse?

It must have been a light of such intensity as to overwhelm his senses. Something so different, so unexpected, that when it came upon him it shocked him in such a way as to lead him to let go of the reins, lose his balance, and eventually fall. What would this light be for us? What could come to us that is so different and unexpected that makes us lose our balance? The answer is perhaps simpler than we imagine and less mystical than some of us would like: new knowledge. Light stands for understanding.

The type of new knowledge that transforms our worlds is that which we were previously unable or unwilling to see. Information that we kept at a distance through ignorance or denial has the power to knock us over. After all, it is easier to slowly sip a cup of hot coffee than to have to drink it all in one gulp. If we take new knowledge in gradually, through our own learning and experience, we are unlikely to be surprised or overwhelmed by it. We can absorb it slowly into our reality, giving us time to process and adapt over time. On the other hand, if we close ourselves to what is in front of us (or within us) for a while, if we refuse to deal with the emotions we harbor for long enough, they come back with the same strength and collected energy we have employed over time to keep them away. Newton warned us of this in his third law of motion: for every action there is an equal and opposite reaction. Although he was describing the physical world, that also holds true in the field of thoughts and emotions. In that manner, our shock and hurt upon being confronted with new information tends to be proportional to the quantity of energy we have employed to avoid or ignore it so we do not have to deal with it and... change.

What knocks us down is having to process, all of a sudden, new information that we were ignorant of or fought hard to deny. What destabilizes us is having to cope with a new reality we could not or did not want to admit in the first place—and that we can no longer postpone facing. It can be a big blow because we are taking it all in at once, instead of doing so through a more balanced diet of gradual ingestion. Perhaps it is the realization that a relationship we care about is heading to its end, that a loved one is reaching their final days, or that other losses are coming: the loss of the job we love or thought certain, the loss of connection to the places and people we grew up with as we move away to somewhere else, or even the loss of the physical ability to do the things we used to take for granted. Hindsight is always 20/20; in retrospect, we often find more details and indications than we realized at the moment. And the reason is simple: we were not paying that much attention. No matter: consciously or unconsciously, we have ignored it—and now we have to catch up.

What can we do, if anything, to prevent that jolt? And if we cannot prevent it, what can we do to mitigate its impacts?

Benjamin Franklin's axiom that an ounce of prevention is worth a pound of cure still holds true today. If we want to prevent the shock that may come with processing big changes, we would do well to invite them in while they are small. By remaining open to change and understanding everything is always in flux, we become more skilled at identifying and handling change.

Openness, however, requires reflection and a new mindset. We must be willing to do it—and we must also spend time reflecting on whether we are actually doing it, if it is going well, and what else we may need to do to make sure it does go well. If that all sounds too abstract, we can bring it to our daily lives in more concrete ways. We can refuse to be entrenched in a routine that traps us in our old habits: we can take a different way home from work every so often; we can try a new restaurant instead of always ordering the same thing from our go-to establishment; and we can experiment with going to the theater instead of the movies, for a change. Whatever it is that you often do, do it differently. You do not have to do everything differently—just enough to invite change and variety into your life. In short: train yourself to constantly adapt to new environments and situations and change, big or small, will seem less daunting. Prepare. Develop the skills before you need them. Flow better through change.

That said, most of us will, at some point, find ourselves in the thralls of painful change before we can realize what is happening—and before we can prepare for it. If that is the case, developing the skills to adapt to change will still suit us in future adventures but may do little to help us at the here and now. If we are already caught in the whirlwind of change and find ourselves devoid of a time machine to go back in time and prepare adequately, few options remain.

The first is to acknowledge that change is happening and that it requires us to make a choice: will we accept it and move through it, or will we fight it to stay how we were? The option is ours—and not choosing is also an option, and one which generally equates to choosing to stay stagnant. If change is here, then fighting it is tantamount to delaying the inevitable—but sometimes a delay gives us time to get acquainted with the idea that we must swim with the current lest it overwhelm us. At times, we need to convince ourselves we tried before we allow ourselves to move on to what is ahead, and sometimes we need that time to let the idea fully percolate within us and the emotions that come with them be properly processed before we are ready to go. No judgement here about what choice you take. (And that includes you not judging yourself either.) Regardless, awareness of the process helps you better withstand it.

A second option is to remind ourselves that this destabilizing moment is also temporary. The discomfort that often comes with changing will not last forever; it will only last for as long as we fight the change. Once we are through it and have adapted, it becomes our new normal and, given enough time, it transforms into a memory of days gone by. In fact, we may find ourselves better off than before after the process has run its course. Still, because we have created the illusions in our heads that things are fixed, we think the pain of changing is permanent too— but it is not. If everything is constantly in flux, so is the discomfort of changing. There is solace in that.

Re-aligning our way of looking at the world is a necessary requirement to processing change as effectively and with as little pain as we possibly can. In fact, change is often about the realignment of mindset to begin with, so if we are able to learn how to constantly process new information and change with it, then we will be prepared to travel down our road to Damascus without falling off our horses (or at least falling less often). This new knowledge, this truth, this light, will set us free—from our own misconceptions. Then we will be truly "enlightened."

TO FALL FROM OUR HORSES

Although the symbolism of a blinding, never-before-seen light shining upon us can be poetic and beautiful, we must remember that it was accompanied by a fall from a horse. If you have ever fallen from a horse, you know this: there is nothing majestic or endearing about it. It is awkward, messy, at the very least disorienting, and, more often, painful. It leaves both a physical mark and an emotional one. You just don't forget it easily. Like falling off a horse, deep change can also be painful.

Pain makes us pay attention and rethink things. One of the stereotypes it behooves us to shatter is that growth and change are always pleasant and grand things. To fall from our horses is to realize that. We sometimes imagine that, when we make an important decision or when we resolve to take on big change, that there will be a choir singing in the background, that the skies will open, that the sun will shine through the parted clouds, that angels will fly down from the heavens with harps in their chubby little hands and it will all be a beautiful moment where we will have so much clarity and certainty about what we ought to do. Basically, that making the decision is the ultimate achievement—ahead of doing the work. Yes, making a decision to change is cause for celebration, but that is not all of it: it is the start of change, and change requires, well, changing. Change requires work. We should be upfront about it with ourselves so we do not get discouraged when we do not hear the celestial voices from heaven and the chubby angels are nowhere in sight.

To put it another way: we all know we must crack some eggs to make an omelette. We often remember the tasty end product, the omelette, but forget that the eggs getting cracked are us: our own misconceptions, assumptions, and old habits. While it is great to focus on the endgame, it is important not to forget what it takes to get there. Otherwise, we will always be surprised by the work it takes to make an omelette when we have to. Simply put, the act of buying eggs does not an omelette make. It still requires cooking.

Nobody really enjoys talking about pain, yet we must—even if for only a little bit. Pain, in all its different forms or manifestations, is likely to take place during our change process when we have not invited change gradually into our lives. And because none of us are at a level where we can foresee everything that can happen to us and prepare adequately, pain or suffering will still be a fact of life. The good news is that, while it cannot always be avoided, it can at least be mitigated.

The best way to mitigate the pain we may find along our way to Damascus is to understand why it is there to begin with and when it can happen. Surprisingly, the why is relatively straightforward: pain surfaces every time something is not working as it is intended. We can take a clue from our physical bodies to better understand the process.

Take the experience of touching a hot stove, for example. We have all done it at some point in time. When we inadvertently touch a hot surface, special sensors in our skin called nociceptors send a message to our spinal cord and then the brain that damage to our body could be taking place. If the brain believes the threat to be a credible one, it creates the sensation of pain so we can direct our attention to the relevant part of our body and deal with the problem. Experiencing that pain, we remove our hands quickly from the hot surface and live to imprudently touch another hot surface another day. This part we may know well. What we often fail to consider is what would have happened were we not to experience pain: if this natural mechanism did not exist, our hand could be severely damaged by continued contact with the hot surface. We are all probably cringing imagining it, but it is true: we could lose feeling in our hands permanently—or worse. Pain saves us from that—when we know how to listen to it. In that manner, the best thing that can happen to our hands (and us, in general) is to feel that pain at that time for that purpose. And address it.

Pain is, therefore, a signal. It is a call to action, to remediation. It is the announcement that something is not working as it was intended and requires our attention—lest we harm ourselves even further. The same applies to emotional pain: we suffer because we are out of alignment with what we want or with what we know should be. When we lose a loved one to death or separation, we often ache because we feel damage was done to us. (For more on loss, revisit the previous chapter, "In a group but alone.") When we regret an action we have taken, we hurt because we know it is out of sync with our moral compass. By knowing it and feeling that pain, we can better safeguard ourselves from being in that position again or repeating the same actions in the future. If we ignore it, it will only fester internally until we run out of space in which to stuff it, and then it will find a way out somehow. When it does, we become human volcanoes spewing hot lava and scorching everything and everyone around us. Would you want to live near an active volcano? So don't be one.

By understanding the "why" of pain we also glean the "when." Every time we are out of alignment with our bodies, our needs, or our consciences, we can expect to trigger pain. The degree of pain will likely be directly related to the degree of deviation from these things: the more damage to our physical bodies, the more pain we will feel; the more egregious our behavior, the louder our conscience will sound the alarm. The art of predicting pain is the art of predicting when we will move away from ourselves, the art of foreseeing when we will not fulfill that which we were meant to be or do. Ultimately, the act of understanding pain and suffering is the process of learning about oneself.

When we look at pain this way, it stops being a liability and becomes a major asset. Whether it be physical or emotional, pain is one of the best mechanisms we have for self-preservation and, more importantly, long-term learning. To see it from that perspective, however, requires reflection and a focus on the big picture—something we are not trained for nor normally inclined to do. Instead, we often focus on the struggle of the moment alone and that is understandably, well, painful. The benefits, however, of grasping the nature of pain and paying attention to its manifestations are immense: we would not be who we are today without the lessons we have learned because pain manifested itself at different points of our lives to alert us to the need to do things differently. For that, we should be thankful. Talk about a 180-degree turn on our perception of pain, eh?

THE HARD GROUND UPON WHICH WE FALL

After we are dazzled by the light and experience the fall, we meet the ground. The ground is where what really matters takes place: it is where Saul feels the pain of having fallen from his horse and has his conversation with the Christ. It has the paradoxical honor of hosting the experiences we least desire and most want; it is witness to our encounter with pain and with a higher calling. So what, symbolically, is the ground? The ground may get a bad rep in our minds and be written off as inconsequential. Yet, at the risk of stating the obvious, it is where all stand. And where is that, exactly?

The ground is the immutable and vast volume of stuff upon which we stand. It is, psychologically speaking, who we truly are—not who we think we are, not who we want to be, not who we think others think we are or want to be. Sometimes, there are too many people in our heads when we talk to ourselves about whom we truly are. The ground is none of that, none of those voices. It is the amalgamation of all the previous experiences, known or unknown to our conscious self, that make up who we are. In that sense, to fall from our horse and onto the ground is to fall back onto our real selves.

We don't often pay attention to the ground because we are too busy trying to fly. We are so intent on moving fast, on achieving, on being something other than what we are, that we can lose touch with what we currently are. When we do, when we trade having our feet firmly on the ground for a horse that can cover great distances faster, we risk losing balance.

Fortunately, we can never fall any lower than the ground—we can never fall lower than who we truly are. We can, however, fall lower than who we *think* we are. So it was in Saul's case: all the comforts and honors his advanced social position bestowed on him also afforded him a horse and a convoy to command. Yet, none of these were *him*: they were attributes of the role he played, which he could temporarily enjoy while in that role. Because he forgot that, when he was exposed to the blinding light of truth, he lost his balance and fell.

We all fall from our horses at times. When we forget that our professional achievements are not who we are, we take our feet off the ground a little bit. When we forget that our social position and the ability to influence others are not rights but temporary gifts, we climb a little higher on that horse. When we forget that our wealth is not an indication of our worth, we risk losing balance. None of those are bad things in or of themselves, but if we are not careful to ensure our feet remain firmly planted on the ground, we risk losing our balance. When we lose balance, we may fall off our horses. That is not to say we cannot climb on horses to get to new places or travel faster. What we should avoid is thinking that is the only way we should travel—or, worse, that we are entitled to always travel that way. To ask those questions of ourselves it to wrestle with our place in the world.

To wrestle with our place in the world is to check to see where our floor is. Indirectly and necessarily, that means asking who we truly are. And who are we, really? When we peel away the complex layers we have placed upon ourselves for work, social acceptance, and our own egos, who are we? When we silence the voices of whom we think others want us to be, where do we stand? (Why is it so hard to bring these masks away from us? What do we think they protect us from?) When our innermost masks come down, who are we and what do we ultimately want? Put this book down for a second and think about it. When it gets hard to cut through the fog, it sometimes helps to think about who we are in the context of what we have done and where we have metaphorically been in our lives—it may help us escape the abstract world of perceptions and assumptions. To know where you stand, it also helps to check the ground under your feet.

To hit the ground is hard work, painful work—and liberating work. It means becoming reacquainted with everything we have done, learned, and been over time. But if we lose sight or notion of where we are or whom we are, life will find a way of bringing us back to it—gently or abruptly. The floor beneath us is the forum in which we wrestle with ourselves, our wants, our wishes, our purpose and meaning in this world. It is the inner sanctum where we dream, yearn, and struggle with meaningful pain. If we lose contact with all of it, we cannot progress—we are just floating around, like untethered astronauts floating in space without a mission. It never ends up well. The floor, then, is where we fight our innermost battles, feel our deepest pain, where we level with ourselves about what truly matters for us.

When we find our balance, though, the ground is also the solid footing that serves as the base for our jumps into even greater heights—and to catch us again when we fall. All of us should, thus, spend time to make sure we feel "grounded." If we want to minimize pain, we need to get to know ourselves better.

WHAT WE LEARN FROM PAUL AND HIS DESTABILIZING MOMENT

When we bring all of this together, the second main lesson we learn from Paul on the road to Damascus is that the unexpected will knock on our door at some point in our lives. With it will come confusion, questioning, and pain. How and when they manifest will be as varied as our own individual circumstances and experiences. Fortunately, these things are not permanent but, rather, important phases we go through on our way to greater personal transformation and growth.

Alongside Paul we learn we must break away from the fairytales in our heads that tell us change is pleasant and clear—because it generally is neither of those things. Change, by definition, is transformation, and transformation can bring with it anxiety, uncertainty, and a dose of pain. Yet we can prepare for change so that our experience is less daunting and less painful—but we will still have to go through it, nonetheless. By understanding the symbolism behind "the light," "the fall from the horse," and "the ground," however, we may learn to help ourselves when doing so. Understanding the whole process helps us focus and get through it quicker.

The first requirement for change is the light—new understanding. We may feel overwhelmed and disoriented when facing the bright light of new knowledge at first—even to the point of losing our bearings—because it is hard to quickly process information we have ignored or refused to entertain. Our degree of shock and confusion will be proportional to the nature of the new information:

the greater the departure from our current worldview and assumptions, the greater the jolt. Yet that is the natural process of evolution: to update our understanding of the world, we must first break free of insufficient notions we previously held. All of it happens amid confusion and doubt.

"The fall off the horse" is exactly that process of realizing that our view of the universe is no longer compatible with our needs or sense of truth—and the pain that comes with it. Always an unwanted messenger at first, pain alerts us that we're out of alignment with our needs or sense of truth and that change is needed, lest we risk even greater physical, emotional, spiritual, or psychological damage to ourselves. As we welcome a new mindset brought about by the new knowledge we acquire through the "light" of new situations, we learn not to run away from pain but to face it, understand it, and address its root causes so we do not find ourselves in need of its helpful counsel again. Negotiating change and the causes of pain leads us ultimately to meet "the ground."

The "ground" is our true and unvarnished self. It is the accumulation of all our experiences, emotions, and thought processes—conscious or unconscious. It is to this we return when we drop all the personas and masks we create to protect ourselves from our insecurities and please ourselves and others. It is on the "ground" that we truly feel our innermost pains—and it's sometimes the last place we want to be. The experience of returning to our own "ground" can be a painful one when we are far from it; when our heads are too far from where our feet should be, we pay a price. Yet, it is then that we have our greatest moments of self-awareness and true reflection. When we listen to our own voice and shed the unreal expectations we (or others) placed on ourselves, we can be said to be "grounded." We would do well to stay there and not lose our footing on our road to something greater.

In short, Paul's encounter with the Christ was the greatest milestone of his life—and it was a destabilizing moment. His experiences shed light on what we can expect as we too have our own encounter with the Christ —the perfect symbol for rebirth into a new reality and the calling to a higher purpose, whatever we may deem those to be. In that sense, Saul's experiences are a blueprint for all of us who will invariably face a blinding light and a fall off our proverbial horses onto the ground as we try to make sense of ourselves and our place in the universe. As we part with our old misconceptions and transform into new people, we are likely to experience confusion, pain, and doubt. Yet, it bears repeating that construction sites are never pretty—until they become the final product they are meant to be. So too are we on our way to Damascus: a personal construction site where great work is still in progress. One full of noise, motion, and change, trans-forming itself daily—and that is best seen and understood from the higher vantage point afforded to us by examining the experiences of those who have come before us, like Paul. With this new knowledge, we understand that the destabilizing moments that knock us down are also the ones that will lift us up in time.

7

LESSON 3: THE COURAGEOUS QUESTION

Our third stop along the road to Damascus focuses solely on the question Saul asks Jesus during their unique encounter—"What shall I do?"[1]—and the answer that follows. As simple as it may seem at first, the question is laden with meaning and marks a key moment in Saul's journey toward becoming Paul. In just a few simple words, we witness Paul understanding that change is happening, embracing the importance of the moment, and accepting he does not know how to move forward. In that moment, he processes where he has been and where he is, and he asks about what is next. This part of Paul's journey of self-transformation speaks to the doubt we naturally experience when we know change is upon us—and the importance we place on having clarity about how to move forward. How Paul handles all of this uncertainty is a model of how we can tackle the very same questions in our own lives.

Because Paul's experience is transferable to our own,

this moment in his life also symbolizes a key moment in our own journeys: it is not uncommon for us to reach a point in our lives when we feel we need to do something different than what we have been doing, yet we do not know what that is or what shape it should take. Without knowing how to move forward, we do one of two things: we either stay put where we are amid the confusion and uncertainty of where to go next, or we return to where we have been before, because that is familiar, clear, and known. Neither of those do us any favors in the long run. Yet we often chose one of them because the way forward is nebulous and unclear. If we cannot see ahead, we tell ourselves, we should not go. In short: because we are not sure of exactly what to do, we do nothing. Thus, the change we have accepted and embraced is postponed— sometimes indefinitely.

We may have seen this play out in our own lives: maybe it is that unfulfilling relationship we find ourselves in but do not leave for fear of not finding a better one; perhaps it is that unsatisfactory career or job we do not quit because we are unsure about what to do next; or possibly it is that trip or move to somewhere you have never been that you put off because you don't know what you are going to find. Whatever it is, it generally revolves around the hesitation of not clearly knowing the specifics of what is ahead of you. What should we do? Because of our innermost fears and insecurities, we only want to trade in certainties: we only want to swap what is known for what is known—even if we do not like what is known. Better the devil you know, they say—but is it? Trading the known for the unknown can be very hard. We leave the unknown out of consideration because we consider it incomplete and insufficient. So we stall.

What then, can we learn from Paul about this key moment of uncertainty in our lives? What answers does he find to the essential question he poses to the universe? His existential question is our question too—and perhaps it never has been as relevant as it is today, in our modern times, when we have more comfort and free time than we have ever had in history, and yet struggle mightily with meaning and purpose. Interestingly, the answer is as telling as the question: "Arise, and go to Damascus; there you will be told everything for you to do."[2] And so he does—and we follow in search of meaning and purpose for our own lives. Shall we go deeper?

PAUL'S STORY: THE COURAGEOUS QUESTION

Saul has just fallen off his horse after feeling dizzy and now finds himself on the dusty ground of the road to Damascus. He is confused. The fall was painful. For a second he is not sure of what just happened. As he tries to make sense of things, that shining light—different from anything he has ever seen or felt—is still there, hovering over him, immersing him in a different reality. Everything around him disappears. A voice then asks: "Saul, Saul, why are you persecuting me?"[3] Saul, trying to make sense of it all, asks for more information. After all, who or what could that be? He has an inkling, but he needs to know for sure. The voice reveals itself to be Jesus,[4] whom Saul has persecuted indirectly by chasing his followers.

In a brief second a flood of thoughts, memories, and conjectures rushes over Saul. In the course of just one moment, he reconsiders his entire life, the experiences that have led him to where he is, his beliefs, and everything he has held to be true and right to that point. This is more than an intellectual exercise and, he feels, more than a momentary whim. What is happening right now to him is incompatible with what he has planned; it goes against what he held as certain; it runs counter to who he thinks he is and ought to be. That moment... that light... that voice... that presence... it negates everything he has built. Everything needs to be left behind. But what to do now? And how to do it?

For another second his mind races on: this time, searching for the way ahead, running through all the possibilities, trying to understand how to reconcile what has been with what needs to be. None of it fits; none of it comes together. There seems to be no rescuing of his past to fit his future. There is no clear path ahead— other than knowing that where he was going will no longer work for him. This experience demands an incredible sacrifice: leave everything he has built behind to embrace something new. Something that he is uncertain of.

Taken by the uniqueness of this experience and feeling the gravity of this moment in his life, Saul replies: "What shall I do, Lord?"[5] *It is the only thing he can do at this point. He does not know where to go from here. And he is before a presence more momentous than anything he has seen or felt before. It is greater than him, so maybe it has answers, because he does not.*

The answer he receives, however, is not at all as revealing as he would hope for: "Get up," said the voice, "and go into Damascus. There you will be told all that you have been assigned to do."[6] *And there we leave Paul: on the ground, hurting and dirty from the fall off his horse into the dusty terrain, shaken to his core, unsure of what is ahead, but told he should keep going—much like all of us.*

OUR LESSONS: QUESTIONING MEANING AND PURPOSE

Paul's existential question has never been as timely. We have come a long way since Saul's meeting with Christ 2,000 years ago, somewhere between Jerusalem and Damascus. Knowledge has grown steadily and then exponentially over the last centuries, affording us comforts never imagined by Paul and his travel companions. Take the journey he undertook in a week or two: today, it would only take us a couple of hours to cover the same distance inside a vehicle with cushioned seats, climate control, and (depending on the company) good entertainment—including music magically coming from invisible radio airwaves or from the fantastic communication boxes we call cell phones. In fact, in under a day we can now fly halfway around the globe to places Paul did not even know existed. And unlike our ancient traveling caravan, we have choices as to what to eat, where to sleep, and, more surprisingly, what to do with our free time. Yes: free time, something we take for granted but that only recently has been made possible to us as technology and science have advanced, allowing us to spend little time doing tasks that would otherwise have consumed our entire days in bygone eras: foraging for and preparing food. Imagine the mind blowing experience our ancestors would have in the frozen food section of a modern supermarket or at an all-you-can-eat buffet. And let's leave medicine, anesthesia, and indoor plumbing out of this—that would be rubbing it in. The world is a much kinder place to us now than it has ever been before.

In short, we live quite the pampered life compared to living conditions thousands (or even hundreds) of years ago. Yet all the facilities and free time we now enjoy have not necessarily made us happier. Everywhere we look, people are struggling with what to do and who to be. While our current lifestyles would be beyond anything our ancestors may have dreamed of in terms of comfort, suicide rates are at all-time highs. Some of us are choosing to take our own lives in hopes of ending the pain created by a void in our hearts. (If only all of us could feel and know the road to Damascus will get better!) Simply put, never in the course of human history have we struggled so much with meaning and purpose. Never have we had so much and felt so little. Having our basic needs met has not led us to happiness—in fact, it may have given us more time to put it to question. Whatever the reason, technology and progress have not delivered on the promise of a more fulfilling life. All of it has left us wondering, like Paul, what we should really do.

ASKING THE QUESTION(S)

One of our first takeaways from Paul's experience at this stop along the road to Damascus is the actual asking of the question. At first glance, Paul's question may seem simple enough: "What shall I do?" Yet, at closer inspection, it goes deeper: it is not just about the general idea of change, but also about the specifics of it. If we dive into it a little bit further, we see it is a question with two levels, so to speak. Let's dissect this for a brief moment.

Let's say a "level 1" question is a big-picture question,

one that starts the decision-making process. An example would be: "should I do this?" A "level 2" question probes deeper into the details of the thing at hand. An example of a level 2 question would be: "how do I do this?" Generally speaking, level 1 questions are wider and broader, while level 2 questions are narrower and more focused. In a linear world, level 1 questions come first and level 2 questions follow from level 1 answers. When it comes to making important decisions, it is good to be able to identify and differentiate level 1 from level 2 questions. It helps us understand why and how we are making decisions.

Paul's question to Jesus is a complex one because it does two things at once: it asks for validation of a decision he is making and how to move forward once that is established. That is to say: it is a level 1 question because he is asking whether to undertake change and, at the same time, it is a level 2 question because he is seeking guidance on how to do it. This is a key moment for Paul and he, understandably, is mired in doubt. He does not know the *what* or *how* of change; everything is up in the air. Who among us has not had a moment of inner questioning like that?

ONE BEFORE TWO: CONVICTION BEFORE CONVENIENCE

When it is hard to navigate doubt and confusion, it behooves us to follow a simple linear process: get an answer to your level 1 question before working on your level 2s. Yes, we will need answers to both; we will need to make up our minds about whether we *want* to change and then figure *how* we will do it.

Yet we must resist the temptation of weighing the *how* in determining the *whether*. It may seem prudent at first to do so: to only move on that which we know how to accomplish. Yet prudence will not breed progress. If the key factor in deciding whether to change is knowing how to do it, then we will never undertake great change of our own volition. Science would never move forward and discovery would never take place if we needed to have it all figured out before moving forward. By its very nature, change is uncertain. To change means to do things differently—and that often includes doing things in ways we have never done them before. And doing things we do not know how to do—yet. Welcome to the uncomfortable zone: the area in which progress and learning take place.

Further, if we are really going to change, we ought to know why we are doing it. We need to listen to our innermost selves and ask our level 1 questions—and get our level 1 answers. Once we have them, then we can move to our level 2 thinking. If we do not tackle our level 1 questions ahead of our level 2, our decisions will be made out of convenience and not conviction. Decisions made out of convenience are fine—but they are never fulfilling or inspiring. They are practical and, well, convenient! But decisions made out of conviction and desire are inspiring and fulfilling. Convenience may be fine for small decisions, but shouldn't our biggest moves be dictated by conviction?

Regardless of how we decide, we ought to be honest with ourselves and know why we make the decisions we make. It is OK to make decisions because of convenience. Not every decision needs to be made out of conviction: what yogurt you eat, what shoes you wear, where you vacation can all be a matter of convenience. The big choices in your life, however, probably should not. You decide what those are. (Maybe yogurt, shoes, and vacations are a big deal to you. That is OK. Just know what your convictions are.) What can become troublesome in the long run is to opt for convenience and call it conviction. If we do so, we risk standing for nothing other than our immediate comfort. That too is OK if we are honest with ourselves, but we may have to face our own conscience down the road when it again asks us to do something different because meaning and purpose is lacking in our lives. When we are dishonest with ourselves, it becomes harder for us to find the fulfillment we seek—because we are hiding it from ourselves. Still, the choice remains ours: do we want to live a life of convenience or one driven by purpose? Paul chose the latter. What will you do?

THE COURAGE TO ASK

Asking ourselves big, level 1 questions, it turns out, can be harder than we expect. Many times, just asking is an accomplishment in and of itself. It takes a certain degree of bravery to stop ourselves, accept that not all may be as well as we would like it to be, and ask ourselves big questions. Paul's courage lies in exactly that: he does not avoid the questions. He faces them with all his heart, mind, and soul—then he acts on the results of his reflections, even if he is unsure about where they may lead him. At the risk of getting too metaphysical and start to ask questions about asking questions, can we honestly say we do the same?

Asking the question of whether we want to change is hard enough. Yet it will be of little use to ask the question and not heed the answer. It's one thing to struggle to find an answer to our level 1 questions; it's another to have the answer and not act on it. Sometimes we even keep asking the same question over and over again hoping to get the answer we want—an answer that will let us stay comfortable. (We must be constantly vigilant against convenience.) None of these are the scenarios we truly want for the long run. So, we must take a moment to be honest with ourselves, take a deep breath, channel some of Paul's courage, hold his mirror to ourselves, and ask: where are we in the process? Have we asked our level 1 questions? Have we gotten our answer? If not, what will it take to get an answer? What is preventing us from doing so?

In theory, asking questions is a very simple process. But when the questions are deep, it becomes a very taxing exercise because it can unearth our own inadequacies and challenge our sense of identity. Sometimes we even struggle with struggling: we may even begin to put ourselves down because we cannot answer our own simple questions. So, if you have been struggling with getting answers, give yourself some grace: you are doing some serious work here. You will figure them out—and that is why you are here on this earth. And there may be some tips we can learn from Paul here too. A key one is vocalizing those questions out loud—and preferably to someone else.

CLIMBING OUR OWN WALLS

Everyone has their own wall to climb. Sometimes we need a little push to get ourselves over the top. For some, "analysis paralysis" is real. Maybe because we feel unsatisfied with the amount of information we have with which to make a decision, or perhaps because we cannot see a clear outcome, sometimes we sputter and stall. At other times we dwell in the confusion of it all because we think we somehow deserve it—and thus, we get stuck in our own "pity party," an event that takes place in our own heads every time we rationalize that the pain and agony of the moment serves us right. There is such a thing as *overthinking* and *overfeeling* the issue, however. It may bear reminding that you are neither the least intelligent nor the least worthy individual to ever come across a challenge like yours. Lesser people have done so, and found their way too. So, why not you? For that, you will need to move, though. The good news is that we can give ourselves that very push we need, whatever the reason we are stuck in a moment or decision. One way of doing it is asking the question with which we are struggling out loud.

When we vocalize the question we are facing, we give it life outside of ourselves. By manifesting it vocally, we extricate it from our brains and bring it into reality. We invite it into action by setting it in motion—and motion is what we want when we are stuck. Urgency and immediacy are kicked up a notch, and now we must move forward to address it, like an archer who only has one arrow and who has to chase it down once it has been shot. There is also a form of emotional release that can take place: when you share your question out loud with the world—even if no one else is listening when you say it—it is no longer just your burden. It may seem silly at first, but try it: get it off your chest.

Better than just vocalizing your question is vocalizing it to someone you trust. If manifesting it out loud brings it to life, sharing with someone both lessens our emotional burden and brings a new level of accountability. If that is not enough reason to do so, consider this: you may also get a different perspective to help you get unstuck. The key to it all is finding someone you trust or respect, though. It may prove unwise to ask for advice from people who are not equipped to give you good insights. Don't ask for tax advice from your mechanic, don't ask for medical advice from your banker—you get my drift. In fact, a good way to choose someone to seek guidance from may be to ask yourself two questions: (1) do they have subject-matter expertise on the topic?; and (2) Do you think they have your best interest at heart? Even if the final decision on how to move forward will remain yours and yours alone (see chapter 1), it may benefit you to get input from those who are qualified. No surprise counseling and coaching have become ever more popular in the modern world: we all can benefit from some thought partnership. It helps to have someone with whom we can share our burdens and who can help us process our thinking.

If you still find it hard to share with someone you know, and you are spiritually or religiously inclined, you may use a tool that has been leveraged for millennia: prayer. Not the formulaic repeating of memorized words, mind you, but an intimate conversation with whatever

force for good you believe to exist beyond yourself. That
sincere act of reaching out and externalizing your questions and concerns may prove as cathartic as a conversation with someone you know. It may also help frame your
questions and thoughts in a way that will lead you to
landing in the answer you are seeking.

Paul did both things in that key moment of his life: he
vocalized his doubt and he sought advice from a trusted
source. And if you struggle with the mystical nature of the
story or with the acceptance of the Christ figure, substitute it for his higher self. Symbolically speaking, it still
goes to the core of the issue here: we need to make time
for reflection, have the courage to ask, and take responsibility for following through. By doing so, Paul definitively
displayed a bias toward action.

A BIAS TOWARD ACTION

Having the courage to ask the difficult question unleashes
us toward action. After all, it will do us little good to live
perpetually in "analysis paralysis" mode. At some point,
we must set the wheels of action in motion. We have
already explored how we must be prepared to make the
big decision on our own. Now we put those concepts in
motion and take responsibility for our next steps, much as
Paul did. How Paul asked his question is a good example
of how to move to action even when you do not yet have a
fully functional plan for getting from point A to point B in
your life. Interestingly, Paul's bias toward action can be
seen in both how he asks his question and in what he
does not say. Let's dig a little deeper.

One of the fascinating aspects of Paul's conversation with Christ is that he jumps into the question of what to do immediately after he ascertains to whom he is speaking.[7] Even after he knows he is speaking to Jesus, Paul does not engage in explanations. Think about it: after he realizes that the figure to whom he is speaking is indeed the person who had started the movement he devoted the latest part of his life to fighting, and that this figure is powerful enough to knock him off his horse and speak to him from beyond the grave, Paul does not dwell on excuses or defend his actions—actions that have led to the condemning and death of many of Jesus's early followers.

Quick confession: if I were in Paul's shoes (or sandals, in this case), if I found myself at the mercy of something clearly more powerful than I could ever imagine, who I had violently opposed to the point of having some of his friends killed, I would be worried. Very worried. I might immediately blurt out a sentence or two about how I did not know what I was doing, I did not understand who he truly was, please forgive me, I thought I was doing the right thing... It may be that I would not be alone: I believe a fair amount of us would display similar behavior. Yet, Paul did not. He knew that would do him little good.

The point here is that we spend significant time and energy justifying our past behavior—to others, but mainly to ourselves. We may tell ourselves we are explaining it to others, but it is really an attempt at feeling better about what we have done or not done. While apologizing for our mistakes should always be high on our list, dwelling on our reasons for making them takes focus and resources away from being and doing better. Words are nice, but actions tend to be the best way to truly make amends for our offenses.

Raising an eyebrow to that argument? Imagine this: you are throwing a party at your house and have invited many of your friends and acquaintances. Out of the kindness of your heart and because you (probably) are in the "host with the most" category, you have provided drinks and food for your guests. During the course of the evening, one of them trips and splashes his or her red wine onto your cherished and pristine white fluffy carpet. (You know, that one you really care about?) What would you prefer he does? Would you rather have him continuously repeat his apology, have him say "I'm sorry" once, then start drinking again near the carpet, or have him immediately bend down to help you clean the carpet as he apologizes? The first scenario can be annoying and leave you frustrated, the second unhelpful and make you wonder if he even really regrets it or not, and the third is the most kind. Even if your friend (if he still is your friend at this point...) is unable to clean the carpet on the spot (pun intended), taking action best displays his desire to truly remediate the problem. Actions always trump words.

Likewise, Paul's immediate question to Jesus—without a perceived pause for explanations or subterfuge—is the best indication that he has taken it upon himself to change and make amends for the damage he has caused. It shows that, in his heart, the need for change is weighing so heavily that he can no longer delay it. There is no time to dwell too much in the labyrinth of words. He must act. He has accepted personal responsibility for the decision and is eager to move forward.

Another piece of evidence that Paul has taken upon himself the responsibility of moving forward is how he asks his question. Notice it comes out in the singular and not in the plural: it is "What shall I do?" and not "What shall we do?" Faced with a force of supernatural magnitude, he could have taken the moment to enlist it to do what he felt needed to be done. Clearly, Jesus would be able to carry the load himself if he wanted—or at the very least carry a good chunk of it. Paul, however, understands that the journey is his—and not Jesus's. He needs to walk the road himself. How many of us would maybe try to make it easier on ourselves by getting someone else to do some of our work for us? Paul does no such thing. He knows that you cannot outsource your key decisions.

As Paul's certainty is crystallizing within himself, we see evidence of his bias toward action one more time when he asks about what to *do* instead of what to *think* about. Given all the doubts swirling in his mind during that short-lived encounter, it would not be far-fetched for him to ask whether he should change his ways. He does not. It seems that he already has his level 1 answer; he wants to change and only needs a nudge in the right direction and some help figuring out where to go from there. At this moment of his journey to Damascus we witness Paul's mental transformation: he moves from shock to doubt, and from doubt to conviction. Much as we will when we have the courage to ask the essential question within us. Action is next.

THE COURAGE TO LISTEN

Once we muster the courage to ask, the courage to listen must follow. Everything Paul has done up to this point teaches us how to move from doubt to action—but he is not done yet. Paul shows us that it is also important to listen. While having the courage to distill our doubts into questions and launch them into the world is extremely consequential, making space for reflection and feedback is also important. A question begs to be answered. It simply is not complete without one—much as we are not complete until we reach our Damascus. We have made progress if we have reached the questioning phase, to be sure. But if all we do is to stay there, then we are not moving forward. If that is so, we are preventing ourselves from fulfilling the incredible potential that lies within us.

As a society, we struggle with listening. Listening, however, does not mean doing what others suggest. Nor does it mean hearing without paying attention. Listening means seeking new perspectives and making space for them in our reflections. In a roundabout way, listening means opening the door to new facts and considerations and inviting them into the parlor of our minds—but not ushering them straight into our mental living room or sleeping quarters. Only after we spend some time engaging with new facts and perspectives and make sure they are sound should we invite them further into our mental home. That time is called reflection—a habit that has rapidly disappeared from our modern lives as we shift from thing to thing at the speed of light.

Listening requires reflection—otherwise it yields little

to us. It all starts, however, with opening the door to new information. Listening is the process through which this intake begins. In that sense, true listening is not a passive action but a highly proactive activity, one that requires courage and practice. Fortunately, when we have had the courage to ask the question and deeply care about the outcome, it becomes easier to have the courage to listen, because we understand what is at stake and why we are doing it. To arrive at an answer, we must listen, both to others and to ourselves. Without listening, we will continue to ask our question out loud into the wind and never grasp the answer.

ARRIVING AT AN ANSWER

Finally, an answer! The purpose of asking the courageous question is to arrive at *an* answer—even if it may not be *the* answer. It is only natural that, after we go through so much effort to squeeze our entire universe into a ball and roll it toward that overwhelming question,[8] we may want a clear and definite answer. The answer we get may not be the answer we want, at least at first—but it generally is the one we need to move forward. As we are still mid-journey, is it even realistic to expect a final answer to all our challenges at this point? That ideal, final answer is Damascus itself—and we are not there yet. We still need to walk some more to get there. So, for the time being, we must prepare ourselves to get *an* answer and not *the* answer—and not let that dampen our enthusiasm. In fact, partial answers may be what we need at this point, lest we be overwhelmed by the long road ahead and discouraged from walking. Let us look at Paul's example again to flesh it out further.

If we reflect on the answer Saul gets from Jesus on the road, we find it telling but not all-revealing: "Get up," said the voice, "and go into Damascus. There you will be told all that you have been assigned to do."[9] It may not seem, at first, like the answer we would like for ourselves; it lays a way forward for Paul, but it falls short on revealing what will happen to him. Thinking about it, however, the answer he gets makes perfect sense for the moment he is in, and it is what he needs to start his journey. Among other things, this answer gives him enough to shift his questions from level 1 to level 2 without encumbering him further. Simply put, the answer he is presented helps him with the next steps: Paul needs to stand up from the confusion and doubt he has dropped into after falling off his horse (again, symbolism...) and keep moving forward even if he is not completely clear to what end. Waiting in the middle of the dusty road to Damascus, dazed and confused, will not do him any good. If he moves forward, however, future clarity is promised. In modern terms, Paul's GPS can only see the first step of turn-by-turn directions, but not the full route at once. He must pay attention to the next turn only, otherwise he risks missing his exit and getting lost in the traffic while inspecting the whole route ahead.

Thus, in the same manner should we prepare ourselves to find partial answers as we trek forward on our own roads. What may seem like a lack of detail about what lies ahead in the distance may indeed be a blessing: by focusing on immediate next steps, we are gaining momentum for the longer walk without being over-whelmed by the full picture. Having just cleared a moment of doubt as we strive to answer our level 1 questions, would we want to engage in it again about all that is yet to come? Partial answers, in that sense, are blessings—even if they may still unsettle us. They may help us focus on what we need to for the time being. Let us also remind ourselves that it is better to have partial answers than to wander aimlessly because we have no answers at all. Thus, we proceed.

WHAT WE LEARN FROM PAUL AND HIS COURAGEOUS QUESTION

Thus we find ourselves at the third stop along Paul's road to Damascus, where we learn much about the power one courageous question may have in our lives. We get here and start with Saul on the ground after his fall, hurting and confused, and end with Paul getting up and with a new purpose. In between, he grapples with doubt, fear, and meaning as part of his transformative encounter with higher awareness, symbolized by the Christ. Again, his story is not unlike our own when we look at the core of it.

Since the best way out is often through, we too must ask the same courageous question Paul did when faced with impending change: what should we do? In reaching for our own answers, we must prioritize conviction rather than convenience—and we must be clear with ourselves about our motivations for reaching the answers we do. If we are not honest with ourselves about the process, we risk wandering aimlessly on the road, trapped in the fear of changing and moving forward, only postponing the inevitable rendezvous with ourselves that must take place if we are to move toward our own Damascus. As it turns out, knowing oneself is a requirement for growth.

Like Paul, the moment we develop the courage to ask ourselves the big question is when we begin to take the reins of our new future. It can be a scary and daunting endeavor, however; as we process where we have been and acknowledge that we do not truly know how to proceed, we are often forced to face our own inadequacies and inner challenges. So hard is it at times, in fact, that we sometimes struggle bringing the question forward from within and often get stuck in the quagmire of "analysis paralysis" or trapped in the labyrinth of "pity parties." Yet we must find a way to overcome these challenges and tend toward action. If not, what is the alternative? Stay confused until the end of our days?

We learn with Paul that it may help to force the question out of our minds and into objective reality by simply asking it out loud and enlisting the help of a trusted source with subject-matter expertise to help us process our choices. Paul has the Christ and so do we—regardless of whether we believe in an external spiritual figure or in an internal higher self or conscience. Whichever way we lean, we have the tools to ask the question—and move forward.

In asking courageous questions, we are led to the realization that we must also open the doors to new perspectives or risk not finding the answer to our dilemma. When we develop the courage to truly listen to people and circumstances around us, we gather vital new information that may propel us toward a new way forward. We learn to listen judiciously, taking it all in but processing on our own, not just merely accepting any path that may be suggested to us—because they cannot truly be our own unless we choose them.

Ultimately, when we have finally willed ourselves out of confusion and doubt for a second to ask the courageous question that has been burning in our souls, we arrive at an answer. The universe always replies to our queries, even if at first the answers we get may not be those we wished for. Still, now that we have ears to hear, we are able to make sense of the answer we will invariably receive. Like Paul, we must pick ourselves up from wherever we are and move forward in our quest for something better. Even if we are not completely sure of all the details of our upcoming journey, the way forward is the way for us—everything else (the details) will become clear later.

So we find ourselves in a new stage of our walk. When we are finally able to go through the process of asking the courageous question that brought us here, when we are finally at a point where we can cast our past and doubt aside to ponder about what is ahead for us, we begin our own transformation from what we were to what we will be. We too begin to change from Saul to Paul in our own ways. All because of a question. In the middle of our own desert, amid pain, fear and confusion, we get up and move forward onto the next stages of our journey. Paul walks ahead of us, showing the way.

8

LESSON 4: THE TEMPORARY BLINDNESS

Our fourth stop along the road to Damascus has us explore the blindness that befalls us when we embrace significant change in our lives—and how we must adapt to the new circumstances it imposes. When we commit to meaningful change and begin to chart new territory, the silent companions—confusion and uncertainty—that journey with all of us often speak with a louder voice. As we contemplate a new path before us, this is their moment to shine as they attempt to hijack our resolve to do things differently. *Should we really do this? Will it work? What am I thinking?* These are the types of questions that echo in our minds.

How we adapt to the new challenges and overhaul our perceptions of the world will dictate how successful we will be in silencing these inner critics and how expeditiously we will arrive at our desired destination—how soon we will be able to "see" again, so to speak. Paul was able to do so remarkably fast, and that is why we look to his example, once more, to learn how we too can handle the apparent blindness that will necessarily follow as we attempt new things.

Change invariably brings confusion. Accordingly, great change ushers in great uncertainty. Whether we are ending a short relationship or terminating a long marriage, adapting to a new reality is a difficult process. Welcoming a new child into the world is life-changing, as is losing permanent custody of children in a divorce. Dealing with the loss of a job leaves us questioning what is to come, just as a new career direction can trigger great anxiety and nervousness. We all are living, have lived, or will live through fundamental change in this lifetime—and witness quite a bit of it visiting those around us. Regardless of what, when, and how, one certainty remains: we will need to adapt to a new way of life. Before we do, we may feel blind, as if we are in the dark. Having lost our bearings, we will struggle with making sense of how we should navigate our new realities so we can again reach a level of psychological comfort. Fortunately, there is good news: it can be done.

As usual, understanding the process and its natural course will help us better navigate and expedite it. That is, again, why Paul matters to us today: we can look to his story of personal transformation to find ways through which we too can overcome the adversities we are bound to encounter. And so we follow, in search of clues...

PAUL'S STORY: THE TEMPORARY BLINDNESS

Saul is on the ground, recovering from the most impactful event of his life. The desert sun strikes his dusty face, calling him back to reality. He has just had a mystical encounter the likes of which he could never have expected or wanted. After experiencing a blinding light, a fall from his horse, and a conversation with the very person he sought to oppose, he is back to where he started. He registers the typical desert smells to which he has grown accustomed in this long journey and senses his horse nearby. He also hears his travel companions coming to his rescue. They grab him by the arms and lift him up, cleaning his robes from the ever-present dust that is unbecoming for someone of his social stature. They ask him if he is OK. He replies he is—but he cannot see them. Or anything else. The encounter with the light has changed him in more ways than one: Saul is now blind. His companions worry: is the blindness permanent? Should they go back? How can he travel in such a state? What will happen next?

As we leave that moment behind us, we should consider that Saul remained blind until he finally met Ananias at an inn in Damascus. The narratives we find in Acts and elsewhere understandably skip ahead to the most important moments, but it benefits us to fill in the blanks to better appreciate what Paul faced on the way to recovering his sight. In between his meeting with Jesus and Ananias restoring his sight, we can imagine the concern of his companions, who urged him to return to Jerusalem (especially now that he was blind); the difficult decision he made to continue; and the hours spent on the long road to Damascus he faced, newly dependent on his remaining travel companion.

In Damascus, we can also picture, he would have made attempts to find hospitality among his many political contacts in the city—who must have refused a changed Saul who now spoke of a new life and a meeting with the infamous dead prophet from Nazareth, the very figure the governing political establishment had struggled to eliminate. Unsuccessful in finding either a supportive listener or shelter, Saul was eventually left by his companion (probably at his own request) at a nondescript inn with little money and nothing to do but hope that his condition would improve. There he sat, blind, until the man he was persecuting arrived and returned his sight.

OUR LESSONS: ADAPTING TO THE BLINDNESS THAT WILL COME

Every decision to change is followed by a period of symbolic blindness. Interestingly, Paul's temporary blindness on the road to Damascus remains largely overlooked by those who are not watching closely (bad puns intended). It is surprising that it is not talked about or focused on more often, given that it is such a powerful symbol. Like many stories of the New Testament, it can be interpreted in different ways, leaving us to decide how deep we want to look. We choose to dig a little deeper because it is so meaningful—and because there is more that we can transfer to our daily lives than a simplistic approach would have us think.

Those inclined to a more traditional religious approach may quickly read Paul's blindness as a test or a punishment from God, while those averse to religion may interpret it as a natural response to the blinding light to which he was exposed. We will take a different perspective and focus on the psychological nature of such blindness as well as its philosophical implications. As we gain greater insight into the temporary blindness that affected Paul, we draw parallels to our own experiences. As we understand why Paul fell blind and how he recovered his sight, we learn how to do the same—allegorically speaking, of course. After all, it does us little good to ascertain the source of pain without working on its cessation. We gain everything, however, by learning how to ameliorate our suffering regardless of its origin.

When we unpack the story, we can see Paul experienced days of blindness, not just mere hours. That is important to remember so we internalize that we too can spend a good amount of time in our own temporary blindness. Days went by when Paul struggled with moving, eating, and communicating with others. Days in which he depended on the kindness of others to go about the simplest of tasks—all in a foreign city where no one he knew would come to his aid. Days in which, without his accustomed ability to see, he lived in isolation, just waiting for something to happen because of a brief and mysterious encounter no one else seemed to understand or believe in. Under those conditions, to say Paul's situation looked dire would be an understatement. Yet, he overcame it; he faced it, persisted, and adapted. And when he did, he recovered his ability to see. But what does it all mean to us?

SEEING BLINDNESS ANEW

Blindness can generally be understood as the state or condition of being unable to see due to genetics, injury, or disease. When we look at it allegorically, blindness can symbolically stand in for a lack of perception or awareness. From the emotional, the psychological, the spiritual perspective, we can be "blind" even when we can physically see.

Paul's blindness is a better guide to us when we understand it as symbolizing a temporary impairment of our ability to perceive and make sense of the world. After we are exposed to critical new information that leads us to reject our old ways of seeing and navigating the world before (how we lived), we are left dazed and confused (so to speak) about what to do next. These are the times when we are told we no longer have a job, when our partner wants to end a relationship, when we are diagnosed with a severe illness—or when we know we simply must change. Such moments are so impactful: we know that we can no longer go on as we did before, but are not sure how to move forward yet. We know we can no longer do things as we used to, but have not yet figured out a better way of doing things. Anxiety, confusion, uncertainty —all of them visit us when we are knocked off balance by the intense light of new knowledge.

IDENTIFYING OUR DAMASCUS BLINDNESS

If we see ourselves in a situation in which we have resolved to change but find ourselves unable to take the next steps, we may be experiencing our own "Damascus blindness." During this stage, we may still be scared of the change we want and the lack of certainty that has presented to us. We may simply not know what to do. Perhaps we are afraid of failing. Because of that, it would not be surprising for us to focus just on our day-to-day, living moment-to-moment, in an attempt to simply run away from that which we know we have to do: move forward. Because we feel we cannot clearly "see" the path ahead, we sputter, we stall, we move in circles, and we can even avoid thinking about it at all. If you find yourself filling up your time with less important things just to be busy and not think, if you are running out of things to watch on Netflix, if you feel you may have reached the end of the internet, you may be in this phase of your journey. Fortunately, we will soon learn that moving forward does not require a clear final destination. We can walk ahead even when we are blind.

Taking all of that into account, we see blindness anew —as the consequence of and the beginning of a needed realignment during a moment of crisis.

CRISES PRECEDE GROWTH

Our temporary blindness often marks the apex of a moment of crisis—whether it be an emotional, psychological, or spiritual one. What we often forget is that crises are not bad things on their own: they are key moments of change. That we have reached a crisis is an indication that we have started the process of change. In that way, it could warrant celebration: we have begun to change, we just might not exactly know all the details of how the change will take place yet. Nevertheless, we are no longer at the beginning of the process but find ourselves halfway. Therefore, rather than focusing on the blindness (or crisis) as a handicap, we should consider it a milestone, a badge of honor. You have made it so far—and that means the odds are in your favor. Facing it as a necessary and important stage in the longer process will help us keep perspective and not get trapped in the difficulty of the moment. To get stuck in the challenge of the moment is to exchange the long for the short term—and a sure way to dwell in pain and confusion longer than we must. Who in their right mind would want that? The best way out of a crisis is the way through—so we embrace it and forge ahead.

THE CLARITY PROBLEM: CLARITY IS NOT SEEING 20/20

One of the reasons we so often get stuck and feel blind is that we unconsciously whisper to ourselves that we need more clarity before moving ahead. Still, progress is possible even when we do not feel we have clarity about what is next. In order words: just because we cannot clearly see a path to our end goal does not mean we cannot move forward. In fact, there may be benefits to not seeing the path ahead in great detail.

For one thing, the road ahead may be so convoluted that seeing it all at once may overwhelm us and make us think of packing up and going back to "Jerusalem" (our home base, our comfort zone) until things get better.

Additionally, what if there are multiple routes you can take to get where you are going? (Who, other than maybe ourselves, says there is only one way forward?) If we were presented with multiple routes all at once, would we fall into analysis paralysis trying to choose which one to take? Moreover, there may be no pre-set road at all, just a final destination to which we must make our own route, a process that may afford us more opportunity to learn. What if making choices about how to proceed each step of the way actually strengthens us? Sometimes, when we are given a clear way of doing something, we do not think of why we are doing it or how we can do it better—we just follow the directions without employing much critical thinking. And if the point of progress is for us to grow, passively following another's path will not get us there.

Without discernment we cannot successfully navigate our way through our road to Damascus. And discernment requires practice. Not having clear step-by-step directions, then, actually helps foster personal growth because it requires us to have our hands on the wheel at all times and be constantly judging and weighing our alternatives. Bluntly put: no cruise control allowed for those who want to go new places. When we think of it this way, we understand that the step-by-step GPS guidance we are looking for is unlikely to exist simply because no one else has really been there before to map the way. It is our road, so we get to map it.

So, the clarity we seek is sometimes the wrong one. The clarity you really need is the one you already have: clarity of purpose. Clarity about the path ahead is unlikely to present itself because the universe lets us make our own path. We will find it at the right moment, but not before it. Understanding that the road ahead of us is a dynamic one is perhaps one of the greatest challenges we will face in our lives. Somehow, the idea that we have to have everything figured out early on (even before we apply to college or decide what we "want to be when we grow up") is becoming more and more a burden nowadays, when we see jobs and careers pop up that did not exist when we were young. The idea that we should have a life plan figured out from the start gives the wrong impression that there is a predetermined path for us to follow. The truth is that there may be a final destination and even some milestones along the way that are highly important for us, but the road we will take to get there is secondary. It stands to reason, then, that we should focus on ideals and goals, not particulars. Particulars and details can always change—without necessarily modifying your end goals. Convictions and goals, on the other hand, tend to have greater staying power.

WHY WE BECOME BLIND ON THE ROAD

Breaking this fixed mindset we have become accustomed to is why the blindness is there to begin with. The blindness we experience on our road to Damascus comes to divorce us from previously established conceptions and perceptions that do not do us any good for the road ahead. Even if they have been helpful for the road behind us, they do not suit us for what is to come—and, thus, like a fire sale at a bad thrift shop, everything must go. Becoming blind means letting go of the way we did things in the past and learning to navigate the challenges of life anew; it means unlearning old behaviors and perspectives that prevent us from growing, from taking the next steps toward greater fulfillment and realization.

If we display what psychologist Carol Dweck calls "growth mindset,"[1] we will invariably have an easier time navigating our Damascus blindness. Having a growth mindset means believing that our abilities can be developed through dedication and hard work. Intelligence, resiliency, adaptability are not predetermined but can be stretched and expanded upon. A fixed mindset, on the other hand, means believing that one's abilities are unchangeable traits.

The distinction between a growth mindset and a fixed one is significant when we compare their perspectives on success: in a growth mindset, failure is an opportunity to learn and grow; in a fixed mindset, because our abilities cannot be further improved, failure is final. In the latter, we shy away from trying what is hard for fear of uncovering we are not good enough; in the former, we are encouraged to tackle what is hard in order to develop our abilities. In short, a fixed mindset limits us while a growth mindset develops us. Simply put, what we want—and need—while traveling on our road to Damascus is a growth mindset. For that, we have to extinguish any trace of a fixed mindset that may be lurking in our minds. This mental purge is difficult and confusing, but it must be done. For the technologically inclined out there, consider it our own firmware upgrade.

Paul was exceedingly good at nurturing a growth mindset, something we see in everything he does once he shifts from Saul to Paul—and which is fully apparent in the speed with which he asks the courageous question we talked about in the previous chapter. Because he was so adept at leveraging a growth mindset, Paul was able to compress the schedule of his (figurative) travels to such an extent that he accomplished in weeks what it would take most of us years or even decades. Maybe that is why his blindness was so brief and why ours can last for so long.

If we want to engage the warp drive of change or go into turbo mode in life, we would do well to emulate Paul in this area. We just might have to break a few mental eggs to make this behavioral omelette. That's why our new best friend, our Damascus blindness, is here: it helps us break down and unlearn our own old, unhelpful misconceptions to make space for new thinking that will help us forward. So, let's welcome it instead of pushing it away.

WALKING WHILE BLIND

At times we forget we can still move ahead while we are working on weaving a new understanding of the world and ourselves. Whether we go full throttle or turtle speed while adjusting to our blindness, the important part is to still go. We must find ways to develop the skills we need to make progress, to walk while the work of rebuilding is still in progress.

The good news is that we are not alone in that. The ability to adapt is becoming a highly prized commodity in modern life. More and more, life points us to the fact that we do not need to have all the answers, we just have to learn how to find them. As the world grows more complex, it becomes increasingly challenging to hold all the answers to anything. As knowledge expands exponentially in our modern era, it is clear we cannot be experts in everything. Whereas our parents and forebearers placed great stock on retaining factual information because that was a sign of learning and erudition, today a teenager with a connected device can find answers to factual questions our predecessors never dreamed of in a matter of seconds. Times have certainly changed: at quiz night in a contemporary pub, the geeks and their smart devices would soundly beat the geezers[2] and their memorized knowledge. Technology has given us almost unfettered access to information and has led us to slowly shift our emphasis from storing knowledge in our heads to interpreting and leveraging information—especially because, at the current rate of intellectual progress, facts are being constantly replaced or updated by new ones.

The latest corporate management models and business schools emphasize collaboration and analytical skills over deep knowledge. That is also why our children are being asked to explain how they got to their answers in math class, as opposed to simply using the formulas we learned in the past. A higher level of discernment is required for the modern era—and our lives included. In short, managers of tomorrow must be nimble, quick to respond to changing environments, and be able to find answers to questions that have not yet been asked. Therefore we ask: if that is happening in our corporate environments, schools, and in society in general, why have we not altered our expectations for the skills we should have to navigate life?

If we are to follow the same developing trends in modern management and apply them to our lives, we too will reach the conclusion that the resources we need to succeed in our road to Damascus are not deep knowledge of a subject matter, experience, or clarity about our path, but the ability to figure things out as we go. When we are able to adapt and tackle whatever problem comes our way, we are prepared for anything. If that is the case, why agonize about not clearly seeing the way ahead? Should we not instead focus our energies on learning to walk as fast as we can while blind? If we approach the task with a growth mindset, we may have an incredibly potent recipe for success: continuous learning and self-development without fear of judgement—external or internal.

MAKING WALKING STICKS FASHIONABLE AGAIN

Once we understand the universe has put us in check by taking our established sight away and accept we can no longer do things the way we used to, we start to move from confusion to resourcefulness. As we let it all settle and remind ourselves that this transformation is for our own good, we begin to let go of what was or what could have been. Instead, we choose to focus on what can be. (If a little bit of enthusiasm seeps in, then we are definitely headed in the right direction!) As we do, the anxiety of not seeing gives way to the pragmatism of finding out how to do things anew. Sure, you may not be able to see the world as you once did, but you still live in it and need to navigate it without bumping into the furniture too many times. So, what can we do to help ourselves move forward?

As we embrace the newly discovered limits of our perception, we may begin to see that there are tools and coping strategies we can leverage to aid us. In a manner of speaking, we begin to develop our other senses to compensate for the limitations in our ability to see. Most notably, our hearing gets more refined: we start to hear better than we ever did before. This is not a small lesson for us. After all, seeing is an individual effort while listening is a team sport. We can use our eyes to see things on our own, but we cannot really have a conversation just by ourselves. When we thought we saw clearly, we believed we needed no one else to orient ourselves; now that we are blind, we must accept we could use a helping hand. As we learn to rely more heavily on our sense of hearing, external input becomes more important than ever. If our companions warn us of a hole along the way, we pay attention and change our step. In doing so, we learn we are not as independent as we wanted to think —a great fallacy our modern society seems keen to perpetuate.

Think about it: is it not ironic that we choose to gather in large cities with millions of people around us and try to build our lives in such a way not to need anyone else? Our egos may want us to believe we are fully independent because at some level we equate dependency with fragility. The opposite is probably the case: we are most frail when we strike out on our own, without a support system to lift us, guard us, and inspire us. Were we truly independent, we would not need cities or groups, for that matter; we would all live our best hermit lives in complete isolation, each on our own separate mountaintop free from the pesky influence of our neighbors. It may be a tantalizing idea for a couple of hours or even days, but would you sign up for the long haul? And because in this scenario we would have no free-trade agreements or industrial revolutions to help us, good luck with foraging for food, cooking, harvesting and weaving natural fibers for clothing, and everything else. While you are at it, please drum up your own entertainment. From scratch. When you have the time. You get the drift.

Perhaps this blindness teaches us that we are confusing interconnectedness with autonomy. Autonomy is being captains of our ship, masters of our faith—within the limits of the law of cause and consequence, of course. (You know: "you break it, you buy it." We are responsible for the consequence of our actions.) Interconnectedness is what we need to survive: we just cannot live a meaningful life on our own. All of us want doctors when we are sick, cooks when we are hungry, companionship when we are lonely, etc. In fact, we cannot live at all without other people—a reality new parents discover much too quickly definitely applies to their newborns ("Here's 20 bucks, kiddo! Get your own milk and diapers," said no parent ever...). As a species, we simply would not have made it if we did not gather in groups. We are more dependent on each other than most of us would like to admit. Reliance on each other is exactly what has led us to accomplish so much and achieve so much comfort in our lives.

So why the aversion to interdependence? What if we relished the possibilities it may bring us? (It would at least make family reunions more bearable...) What if our new found growth mindset blessed our efforts to reach out to people who care for us or who are experts in areas we are not well-versed in for advice when we need it? What if, instead of fighting our limitations, we embraced them instead and gathered the information we needed to prop us up when we are hesitant? What if we leaned on each other to steady our own balance in unfamiliar terrain? What if we leveraged each other as walking sticks when we are "blind"? Should we call Louis Armstrong in for a background rendition of "What a Wonderful World" to better make our point?

That was a whole paragraph of questions to say this: let's make walking sticks fashionable again. It is a mathematical certainty, that when we distribute a weight over multiple support points, we arrive at a sturdier structure. Flying buttresses, gothic cathedrals, and architects everywhere agree. It is also good advice for those trying to build something in their lives. A little push from the outside helps us hold up better. We can do the same emotionally, psychologically, and spiritually without ever being the weaker for it. On the contrary, by taking someone's arm when we need it, we make ourselves stronger, faster, and less likely to trip and fall along the way.

Our Damascus blindness helps us break down our erroneous concept of self-sufficiency and teaches us to rely on people again. By being forced to let go of how we saw and understood the world, we are freed to expand our perception. If before we figured we could do it all on our own, afterward we realize we need the assistance of others to walk part of the way—even though we are still the ones doing the walking. If anything else, being blind while on our road to Damascus makes us more considerate and less self-absorbed. Our Damascus blindness shifts our attention outward, forcing us to accept input and help from other people—something our more self-centered selves may not have considered or easily embraced before life pushed us that way. Before his transformational encounter with the Christ, Saul may have been too proud to accept lodging in an inn in Damascus given his elevated social standing. Paul, on the other hand, would never have made it to Damascus without the guidance and support of the companion who helped him navigate the remainder of the way (and, come to think of it, may have had a less pleasant journey). He knew he could not safely see it through by himself. By accepting help, Paul went farther and faster than Saul would otherwise have been able to. So can we.

SEEING AGAIN

Our blindness can be challenging and transformative, but it is also temporary. Much to our relief, eventually we get to see again. Paul had his eyesight restored by Ananias at the inn in Damascus. We too will eventually rebuild our perception of the world—with the help of others. We will see again, but not as we saw before. As we are able to move ourselves from our often monolithic and inflexible ways of going about our business toward a growth mind-set, the anxiety of not being in control and the fear of not having clarity are replaced by an inner confidence that assures us we will be able to adapt to whichever situation comes our way, and that we can leverage the expertise of others to do well. As our own tension and doubt levels drop, a new normal slowly establishes itself. We know we can grow to meet the challenges of the day because we no longer see ourselves as fixed entities with hard limitations and capabilities; we become ever-growing and evolving consciousnesses that gobble up skills and new tools in the Pac-Man-like game of life.

And the good news keeps coming. When we regain our sight, it comes back with greater quality. Because we have expanded our ability to see through our new mindset and perspective, we notice things we had not before. In a manner of speaking, it is almost as if we had laser eye surgery to correct our past limitations. Lasik for the soul, if you will. An example of such improvement is the very growth mindset we have talked about. In this new stage, we are not only able to see ourselves better, as dynamic beings who are constantly changing and growing, but we also extend that understanding to others. That is to say: if we are learning and growing, so is everyone else. Such awareness allows us to be more patient and tolerant of others because we all bear the stamp of "work-in-progress" somewhere in our beings. This powerful awareness can bring a series of benefits that are often too many to enumerate: from better relationships and greater insight into how to help and move others forward, and everything in between.

ROME WASN'T BUILT IN A DAY

While there is reason to be optimistic about seeing again, we should also be aware that our vision will not return quickly. It takes time to transform perspectives and worldviews. It may also take some uncomfortable experiences to help us break down old walls and cement a new mindset. Paul's story, as it is summarized to us, quickly goes from the mystical encounter with that blinding light to the recovering of his eyesight. Let us not ignore, however, that he lived the in-between, even if it is not explicit in the narrative. We too will have to grapple with this period of blindness. Knowing in advance can help us mitigate some of the challenges that will present themselves, but we cannot skip the process altogether. It will still be up to us to live our story, even if no one is following it during those moments. Fortunately, how long this blindness will last will depend on our willingness to embrace the growth mindset and the walking stick we referred to before. That is up to us—which puts us in the driver seat of our destiny.

WHAT WE LEARN FROM PAUL AND HIS TEMPORARY BLINDNESS

Paul's temporary blindness holds tremendous significance for us in the allegory of his journey to Damascus. As one of the outcomes of his destabilizing meeting with the unexpected blinding light of a new reality, his blindness is often overlooked by those who try to make sense of his story. But when we pay attention to this fourth stop along the road to Damascus, we discover a trove of symbolic meaning. It is only by putting ourselves in his shoes and imagining walking the remainder of the road to Damascus without seeing that we better internalize the challenges he faced and understand the work we too need to do.

Perhaps the best place to start when dealing with our own perceptual impairment is to understand why it is happening in the first place. Change requires it. The symbolic lesson we can take from this moment in Paul's journey is that, as we shift our whole being to seek new things, we need to overhaul how we see and understand the world. This process is often unexpected and generally deeper than we had supposed: inner change is not just about doing things differently, but seeing things differently, too. After all, to see differently is to understand differently. If we were to see the world the same way we did before, behave as we did before, and do things as we did before, we would be as we were before—and remain unchanged. Thus, we must expunge from our minds the old operating system before we load a new, more powerful one. The process of upgrading oneself will always be riddled with anxiety. As we wait for the new operating system to load, we sit nervous and uncertain that it will work out—but it does. Even if we have to do it multiple times or wait for a while, it does work out.

Having an understanding of the whole process beforehand allows us to understand what things are happening and why. Knowing that we will have to update our thinking and being aware of the benefits it will bring us leads us to see the blindness anew: not as an incredible barrier to progress or even as a setback, but as a necessary process of growth and transformation that will catapult us forward. From the highest of perspectives, the blindness we experience in retooling ourselves is a remarkable ally. Call it a blessing, if you will. If this idea has not yet settled within, then chances are we are still in the middle of the process, where confusion, uncertainty, fear, and anxiety run high. If these unfriendly detractors are still journeying with you, rest assured you will be able to silence them (nonviolently) in time. Keep going over and over the big picture until it sticks—then notice their voices fade, little by little. You will outlast them. You have prevailed before and you will again.

Yet, developing an understanding of the nature and process of our Damascene blindness is not the same as being clear on what our next steps are. While we may have clarity of purpose, clarity of path will remain elusive because it will be up to us to trail-blaze our way forward, growing in discernment along the way. We can release some of the pressure we may be imposing on ourselves (or others) to have it all figured out before we start moving. In that new reality, factual knowledge becomes something we prize but not obsess about. Instead, we choose to focus on developing the skills to make good decisions along the way. This will serve us well, because the road can be different with the seasons. What we know of the path today may not be true tomorrow. Rather than walking with our heads down all the time trying to avoid the potholes we find on the path and risk missing a turn, we lift our chins and look ahead, trusting our feet will make the right moves in due time to avoid the barriers we spot on the horizon.

Thus, the blindness we encounter on our way to Damascus helps us expand our understanding of the cosmos. It leads us to the realization that we are beings in constant progress and invites us to let go of the fixed mindset we may still hold. This new awareness whispers to us that we can move ahead even if we are still clouded by doubt, because we will adapt and overcome. It also greatly expands our understanding of ourselves and the world, because it puts our egos in check and clarifies that interdependency is not weakness but a fact of life—and something that can actually help us travel faster. No longer scared by the blindness, we turn our minds to finding ways forward and begin to notice our other senses have improved. We begin to hear better and, in doing so, we heed the advice of others. We take kindly to the help of others too and, in doing so, gain a sturdier footing with which to travel the road. In short, our growth mindset leads us to be a more kind humankind.

When we become better at seeking others out and connecting, when we learn to accept help and value others' feedback as important input into our decision-making progress, we see the world anew. At that moment, we realize we have changed. We have adapted to new circumstances which at first we thought to be detrimental but that turned out to be transformational. In short, we are no longer blind: we have regained our "sight" and, surprisingly, can actually see better and farther than we did before.

At the end of it, the blindness that first shocked us has become a great teacher. It has led us to transform how we see ourselves, others, and the world; it has taught us compassion and humility; it has transformed challenges into opportunities for growth; it has developed us into flexible human beings capable of adapting and outlasting any circumstance thrown at us; and it has reminded us we are able to make progress even when we think we are lost. Because the truth is we are never lost; we may not see clearly for a while but, like Paul, we are making progress on our road to Damascus. So we continue...

9

LESSON 5: THE DECISION TO GO AHEAD

Our fifth key learning from Paul's journey to Damascus revolves around making the conscious decision to set ourselves in motion even while we may still be blind. Everything that has happened to Paul while on the road so far has lead us to this key moment: from understanding that although we may travel together, the key decisions about our life will always be our own; to realizing that the moment that call us to awareness and change may not present itself like a fairytale but a painful one; to finding the strength and inner clarity in us to distill our doubts into a guiding certainty about what we really want to do; to eventually embracing the confusion that will arise from shedding old perspectives and learning to see the world anew, it all builds to a fundamental question we must address if we want to proceed: where do we go from here? Will we continue forward toward the Damascus we seek or will we choose to return to the safety of Jerusalem?

At some point, we will have to decide whether we are going to fully commit to changes we have been wrestling with or whether we will go back to our old way of thinking and being. This is the moment when the proverbial sandal meets the road (as there were no rubber soles back then). Up to this point, we have been talking about emotional and psychological concepts. Now comes the moment when we must take everything we have worked on to this point and set it in motion. This is when we decide if and how we will move. How will we put our feet to use? Will our hearts and minds send us forward into what is to come, or will we ask our feet to take us back to where we have been so we can rest in the comfort of the familiar?

This moment will manifest differently for each of us. It could be deciding whether you are going to leave behind that career it took you years to build and pursue something that speaks to you; whether you are going to leave a relationship that does not fulfill you; whether you are going to take that leap to move to a new city for a new job or a new adventure; whether you are going to put your savings on the line to start the new business you have dreamed of; and so on. This is the moment when we make a "go" or "no go" decision. Even though our individual experiences may be different from each other, there are common lessons we can harness from Saul's transformation into Paul.

PAUL'S STORY: THE DECISION TO GO AHEAD

Paul is back on his feet. He has just had the most remarkable experience: a light so intense that knocked him off his horse and onto the ground, where he heard a voice he recognized as that of the very prophet of Nazareth he had set out to discredit. How could that be? Jesus was dead! He, Saul, had been mistaken… In a moment, he knew he had to change. He re-evaluated his life and decided he would go a different way, even if he were not clear about what it meant. So he asked the Light for help and was told to keep going to Damascus—and here he was. When the Light went away, the darkness came. He could no longer see. He could sense the sun, the scents of the dessert around him, he could feel his horse near and, more importantly, he could hear his travel companions. They worried for him. Why should they not? He could not see a single thing, not even a speck of light.

Now what? He hears the worried tone of his travel companions talking amongst themselves about what to do next, worrying that he has hit his head, whether they should turn back. Clearly, they are saying, he is not well.

He is not—yet he is. He cannot see out of his eyes, but his heart has new clarity. He knows he must seek out and teach others about what is divine: to make amends, to start again, to make a difference. But he does not know how, specifically, to do that. Should he keep going toward Damascus, even though he cannot see? His companions are adamant he should return; they say they will not take him to Damascus, that he should go back, that he knows people in Jerusalem who can help him. Maybe, if he goes back, he can rest a bit and wait for his sight to come back. Yet can he go back? Can he return to Jerusalem and face everything as it was? Can he go back to his old life and talk to his acquaintances about what happened? Or not at all? Would they understand? Would he be able to convince them, to show them that their attitude toward the teachings of the prophet from Nazareth was misguided?

He has to decide. They cannot just stay there, in the middle of the road, waiting for his sight to come back. They have already waited for a while and nothing has changed. Shall he return with them back to the comfort of Jerusalem, or shall he risk his health and safety and make way to Damascus? He could use some rest in his own bed, near his servants and friends... But he is already here, on the road, close to Damascus—and there is that new spark in his heart...

No, he will not go back. He cannot go back. He will go forward to Damascus; whether they come with him or not, he is moving forward. So he starts walking...

OUR LESSONS: MOVING FORWARD AMID THE CHAOS

The toughest of choices often take place at the hardest of moments. That is why they are so difficult. When we are unprepared or tired, it is hardest to arrive at a decision—especially one that has the ability to really change our lives. So much so that we often advise each other to "sleep on it." That is: to take our time, to think it through, to factor it all in before deciding. Wise advice, no doubt; but we should not let ourselves confuse pondering with postponing. Our friends and companions are also likely to suggest we stay put where we are before moving in different ways. But what if you have done all of that and still find yourself woefully unprepared to make such a decision? We cannot sleep on it forever. At some point, we must act. We must harness the strength in us to make the best possible choice we can among all the current options —and go.

Making that choice is not easy—nor is it meant to be. Because it is such an important one, with the potential to radically transform our lives, it is one that we should not commit to haphazardly. The struggle gives meaning to it— it creates buy-in from ourselves to ourselves and the road we choose. Yet, it is a grueling process because it tosses us outside of our comfort zone to make a sizable decision that can impact our lives and that of those around us. And we must make it while dealing with other challenges, as we will see. It is contending with so much at once that characterizes this key moment in our lives. It is in this phase, where we hold uncertainty and discomfort in the same space where we are learning to change our perception of the world, that we have to make the decision to go ahead. No easy feat.

No wonder this moment can cause a great deal of anxiety and doubt to those in it. On the other hand, it also offers the excitement of the new and of what can be, if only we learn to look forward. To be in this phase is to recognize the tension that exists in the teetering between these two powerful feelings: fear and excitement. Ultimately, however, we must choose between comfort and growth. Which one shall it be?

Before we decide, let's dive deeper into the mechanics of this moment of our lives so we may better understand the situation in which we must make such a choice.

THE CHALLENGE OF OVERLAPPING LESSONS

Until now, we may have had the impression that the lessons one learns from a Pauline journey to Damascus happen in a linear fashion. That would be ideal and would certainly make things easier, but that is not always the case. As the British-American poet T.S. Eliot reminds us, we may have the experience but miss the meaning.[1] Because having the experience is not necessarily arriving at its lessons—at least not immediately—we may sometimes find ourselves dealing with multiple learning opportunities at the same time. As we delay reflecting on and learning from them, they are pushed farther down the road and can end up overlapping each other. In short, they may pile up. For example: we may not learn our first lessons about being "in a group but alone," ahead of having our "destabilizing meeting" or grappling with asking "the courageous question." We may only come to terms with the fact that we are the only people who can really make key decisions in our lives after we feel the disappointment of not having anyone to help us during that destabilizing moment.

Internalizing the lessons we pick up from Paul's journey in the order in which they present themselves to us would make things easier. But we recognize that each individual brings with her or him a series of previous experiences and habits that may lend them to either breeze through some of these key learnings or require additional time to internalize them. After all, we are all different, learning at different paces and facing different mitigating or extenuating circumstances. We all have our own individual roads to travel.

That is one reason why it is useful to remind ourselves that Paul decided to go ahead amid his own period of blindness. Not before, not after. During. Paul had to make the decision to keep going toward Damascus even though he was no longer able to see where he was going. Had he been able to still see or had his sight been restored already, it would have made for a different decision altogether; making the decision to move while suddenly, newly blind is much harder than doing so with your usual faculties intact. But life-changing decisions often require us to take a stand while we are dazed and confused or, at the very least, wrestling with a high degree of uncertainty. These key moments are so challenging exactly because we cannot see what lies ahead. They test our resolve.

The blindness undoubtedly adds a degree of complexity and uncertainty that leads us to reconsider things. In Paul's particular case, had he made the decision to go ahead after meeting with the Christ and before he became blind, he would probably have had to revisit it after losing his sight. Losing our reference points is so rattling (as we described in the previous chapter) that it tends to consume all the air in the room. It eats up the attention any other topic or important decision would otherwise receive. Becoming temporarily, unexpectedly blind puts our world on pause while we desperately try to see again. Yet we cannot simply sit around waiting for our eyesight to return—because unless we do something about it, it may not. Instead, we must make our way through life much the same way we would navigate a new room blindly: cautiously but moving forward and aware that we may occasionally bump our shins on furniture we cannot see. If Paul had refused to move while he waited for his blindness to heal, he would have certainly starved and perished on the road, not too far from where he had his life-changing encounter with the light and, paradoxically, first became blind. Not exactly the outcome we would want for ourselves, right?

That is an important aspect of this key learning we should pay attention to and that bears repeating: we must often make the most important decisions of our lives while we are struggling to make sense of the world, when we feel we do not have all the information we would like to have. Translating that back into our Pauline framework, it means that two stages happen at once: we are facing both "the temporary blindness" and making "the decision to go ahead" at the same time. They are intertwined and interdependent: you cannot successfully restore your emotional, psychological, or spiritual eyesight without persevering on the road, and you cannot truly move forward unless you have resolved to do so against all odds. The decision to move forward will not automatically cure our blindness, but healing ourselves requires we move ahead, no matter the circumstance. It is the moving that teaches us to develop a new awareness and utilize our other senses. In short: this moment is a "twofer"— a two-for-one package deal. Still, preparing for each lesson independently may give us a leg up when it comes to facing the decision to go ahead.

THE GRAVITATIONAL PULL OF FRIENDS

To go in a new direction requires breaking orbit from our established habits—and relationships. To make matters more challenging, we may also experience well-meaning pressure from our friends to return to our previous "orbit." Apparently, it is not enough to learn how to see the world anew while deciding whether to go forward: we must also cope with peer pressure we may feel from our acquaintances, family members, and friends to return to our zone of comfort. When we think of it, that is not really surprising: it is only normal that they would want us to remain who we are.

After all, that is the person they have known—and liked—sometimes for many years or even a whole lifetime. It is hard for any of our acquaintances to envision us being different than what we are now because who we are is all that they have known. To be fair, it may be that few of our relations have heard about our innermost fears and desires as modern relationships often fail to go deeper than the superficial varnish of acceptability and superficiality we think are hallmarks of modern friendship. (And—without judgement here—not many of us spend a lot of time coming up with new opportunities for personal growth for our friends either. Generally, we are so consumed with our own problems that it is hard for us to get a grip on them, much less proactively think of new opportunities for others. Unfortunately, when we do think of our friends' actions—and just a little bit of judgement here—it is often to criticize them.) So what happens more often than not is that our friends may resist the changes we want for ourselves. They may prefer us to stay where and who we are because that is what they know, and because our changing also transforms their lives. The moment we are different, we leave a vacuum in their constellation of relationships that forces them to adapt—and adapting means changing. Thus, by transforming ourselves we change the gravitational balance of not only our own solar system but that of many others as well. In that sense, to change ourselves is to change the universe, even if imperceptibly.

Why should we expect that others fully support our desire for change if we have not been sharing with them some of our innermost bubblings and percolations? If we have not spent considerable time understanding their desires and wishes and being open to their changing, should we expect they would do it for us? It would be wonderful if they did; it would be a mark of true friendship—but, as we touched on in "In a Group But Alone," we should not expect it. Another benefit of thinking this way is that, when we lower the expectations we impose on our friends, we find ourselves positively surprised if they go beyond them. It's a win-win.

To be clear: we are not casting shadow at all human relations here. We simply wish to make the point that although they are extremely important and rewarding to all of us, our relationship to others cannot determine or lead our desire to change ourselves. We must change because we want to do—not because others think we should. Transformations triggered by our desire to please others are generally not lasting because they lack the amount of sustaining energy required to maintain ourselves in a new orbit. That energy comes from the sheer power of our will—we cannot borrow or steal it. There are no shortcuts when it comes to major change. Before we attempt to change ourselves, we should be clear for whom we are doing it, as it will require much and affect us forevermore.

COMFORT VERSUS GROWTH

It is for that very reason that we need to be clear whether we are choosing comfort or growth. (Emotional safety can be used as a synonym for comfort here.) Ultimately, every decision to change hinges on either the desire for comfort or for growth. The choice is always ours: will we step forward into the unknown to attempt change or retreat to the comfortable and safe? The desire for stability and comfort is a powerful force that beckons us to stay where we are—or seek ways of perpetuating the status quo. They are the antagonists, the couch potatoes within us that would rather watch endless life reruns than try new programming for our lives. If they could, they would never leave the house and stay in pajamas, eating takeout. While there is definitely a place for a pajama day in our lives (and COVID-19 has surely proved it!), staying in them indefinitely may not make the best guiding principle for leading a fulfilling existence. Avoidance and withdrawal may be fun for a couple of days, but deriving meaning from it is impossible. Learning and personal growth require adventuring outside of the house—and not in our PJs.

One interesting way to look at our learning experience is to leverage the model put forth by Soviet psychologist Lev Vygotsky. Although Vygotsky remains less well-known than Jean Piaget, his work on cognitive development has become the foundation for a lot of research and different theories of learning in the past decades. While Vygotsky's (and Piaget's, for that matter) work centered on how children acquire knowledge and understanding through thought, experience, and their own senses ("cognition"), we would not be stretching it too far by also applying it to adults. (After all, growing old appears to be mandatory while growing up falls in the optional category. You know what I mean.) At any rate: Vygotsky placed a greater emphasis on our social environment as an important factor for learning than his predecessors.

According to Vygotsky, social interaction plays a significant role in developing cognition—in learning to make sense of the world. Rather than arguing that understanding the world comes *after* we have developed the internal mechanisms to do so, Vygotsky espoused the notion that such mechanisms were developed by the interaction *with* the world. That is to say: it is by engaging with the world, struggling with different tasks and situations, that we learn and grow. Although scholars believe Vygotsky's work was never truly finished because he died at the early age of 38, what he proposed aligns well with Paul's experience on the road: he did not sit around waiting for his sight to return before taking to the road again. Translating the allegorical gobbledygook into practical terms for us: we should not wait to develop a full understanding of the world or a fully functional plan before venturing forth in our lives. We grow by moving forward and engaging with what's ahead, as we walk.

Let's visualize Vygotsky's concept of learning: Imagine

three concentric circles. The smallest, lying at the center of it all, represents what a learner can do or learn on their own. The medium circle, which surrounds the smallest one, represents that which the learner can do or learn with the aid of others; in this area, which Vygotsky calls the "zone of proximal development" (ZPD), we can learn and grow with the help of a "more knowledgeable other" (MKO). The largest circle, containing both smaller circles, represents that which is beyond the learner's reach. In that sense, Vygotsky's model could give us a handy visual representation of how we learn.

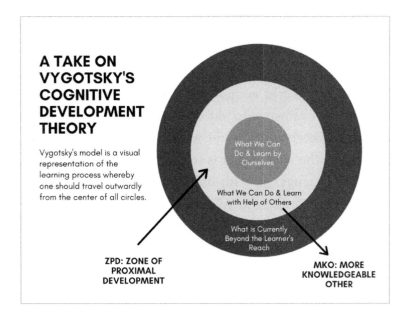

A TAKE ON VYGOTSKY'S COGNITIVE DEVELOPMENT THEORY

Vygotsky's model is a visual representation of the learning process whereby one should travel outwardly from the center of all circles.

What We Can Do & Learn by Ourselves

What We Can Do & Learn with Help of Others

What is Currently Beyond the Learner's Reach

ZPD: ZONE OF PROXIMAL DEVELOPMENT

MKO: MORE KNOWLEDGEABLE OTHER

This visual may confuse the inner Robin Hood within all of us because we do not want to shoot for the bullseye right in the center. What we really want is to operate on the second layer. It is in that area (again, the "Zone of Proximal Development") where, with the help of a "More

Knowledgeable Other," we learn and grow. Besides being fancy terms one can casually drop at a cocktail party to feign sophistication and knowledge, the MKO and the ZPD have another important application: they are at the core of learning within the Vygotskyan paradigm. They express the ideas that we need input from the outside world to help us stretch beyond our current state to grow. We need an MKO—whether it be a person, a life situation, or a light in the desert—to help us do what by ourselves we would not be able to. We need a good teacher, if you will—and teachers come in all shapes and sizes.

At the same time, we must also understand that we have to operate within our own personal ZPD if we are to grow. Attempting to work outside our zone of proximal development will be ineffective. It is likely to be very frustrating too. For the sake of illustration, think of a kindergartner in a college-level physics course: while he or she may physically attend a class, it will neither captivate our little person nor provide her or him with substantial, lasting learning. The lessons taking place in such a class are just too far removed from the kindergartener's current understanding to stick. Bringing it back to more practical terms for us: remember that greater plan with detailed step-by-step directions we want for our lives? Yep, that lives in Vygotsky's third larger circle. It is out of our reach for now.

But not forever. Vygotsky's circles are elastic. Whenever we are able to work in our zone of proximal development and acquire new knowledge or skills, we enlarge our inner circle. Now that we know and can do more, our inner circle is bigger—and our ZPD moves outward and expands too. In this model of learning, the goal is to gobble up any surface you place your circles on top of—like a hungry Pac-Man who grows each time he absorbs the morsels of experience nearest him. That kindergartner we talked about will grow and make her or his way into that physics class, if she or he wants. It will just take time and many MKOs along the journey to expand his or her ZPD to that level.

Learning, then, is constant expansion—and it requires an outward motion into the unknown. In a manner of speaking, Vygotsky's framework is about "thinking outside the box": what we really want is to think, do, and live outside that smallest circle.

DISCOMFORT AND LEARNING

Vygotsky's learning framework leaves us with a couple of important gifts. First, it reminds us that cognitive development takes place both inside ourselves and out in the world. It is a gentle reminder that we should welcome outside stimuli as a necessary and powerful factor for our personal growth. When we have "eyes to see," any person, situation, or circumstance can be that "more knowledge-able other" that teaches us something. We cannot just isolate ourselves from the world until we figure things out, nor can we only pay attention to the outside world. We must balance both. Becoming a hermit isolated from others atop a mountain will not make you a sage, and neither will only following the opinions of your friends. Second, it indirectly provides us with an intellectual basis for hope. Vygotsky's thinking points to the fact that every learning experience can be marked by a degree of discomfort. The bigger the discomfort, the larger the distance from our comfort zone—or inner circle. Therefore, we can use discomfort as an indicator for learning. That is to say: when we recognize that we are in an uncomfortable situation, that is our cue to realize a learning opportunity is presenting itself. That is our sign that we have a chance to grow. That discomfort can be the trigger we need to bring Carol Dweck back to the table and shift our mindset from a fixed to a growth one.

When we do so, a quiet miracle takes place within us: we begin to *feel* that the challenges we face are nothing more than true opportunities for learning. We may have already *told* ourselves that, but spending additional time to fill in the blanks between that statement and the rationale for the statement can help us connect our minds to our hearts. (Connecting our minds to our hearts is the longest 20-inch journey we will ever take. Sometimes, it is the shortest distances that require the longest journeys.) The more we support the idea that challenges are learning opportunities with rational evidence, the more we believe it—and the more we believe it, the easier it is for us to feel it and to act it out. Sitting Vygotsky and Dweck at the same table helps us establish that connection between reasoning and feeling.

Applying Vygotsky's framework for learning further can explain Dweck's assertions about the two different mindsets. Perhaps we have tried to jump from our innermost circle to our outermost one without doing proper work in our ZPD and failed. (Maybe even repeatedly, as we attempt the same thing many more times.) And in failing, we taught ourselves we just did not have the skills or smarts to get to expand our rings. So we stopped trying. We told ourselves a lie and believed it.

Now that we understand we need to take the time to work in our zone of proximal development to properly learn and advance, we see failure is not final. Instead, we understand it as an indication that we have not yet mastered all the components or skills required for succeeding in that particular lesson. That realization is akin to pulling the curtains open on the Wizard of Oz[2]—it kills the myth. Failure is our cue to awaken the Sherlock Holmes within all of us, backtrack a bit, and reflect on the intermediary steps we may need to take or the abilities we may need to nurture to get to that next stage. It is (almost) elementary, my dear reader.

THE POWER OF FAILURE

From that perspective, we are prepared to make a wild assertion that turns our society's current thinking on its head: failure should actually be more prized than success. Failure is diagnostic, it gives us direction; it points to what we can work on next. Success is just a status; it may tell us where we have been, but it does not really tell us where to go next. Success is backward-facing, while failure is forward-facing. Success tends to keep you in your innermost Vygotskyan circle, suggesting that you should do the same thing over and over again because it worked. Failure, however, points you to your zone of growth and says, "Let's get it. Let's do something new." Success also has a deceitful aspect of which we should be wary: it invites amnesia. If we are not careful, success makes us forget that it took learning and effort to succeed—and that includes failing along the way. Success can also be a master of illusions. If we are not careful, it can feed our ego. If we do not keep ourselves nimble over time, success can become the ultimate trap: one that keeps whispering to us that we need not do anything differently because we have already figured out everything we need to figure out.

History shows us that civilizations have fallen exactly because they bought into this myth that success means you don't need to learn anymore. Because they were too comfortable in their own skin, they are no more. That is why most of the world does not speak Latin anymore as it once did, and why the sun now sets on the British Empire —to name just two examples. We even have a term making the rounds in business circles to explain that process: "disruption." Bluntly put, the Roman and British empires both got "disrupted" because they lost their ability to "innovate"—which is just a synonym for "try new things." Because they could not fail a little bit at a time, they ultimately succumbed. It is ironic, in a way, that the inability to risk failing in new things is what finally did them in. As a more knowledgeable other, History seems to consistently echo: fail forward or fail finally.

THE EXCITEMENT OF FAILING FORWARD

If success can sometimes be a purveyor of illusions, failure can be a coach. By keeping us focused on what we need to work on, failure can give us motivation and even excitement. Yes, excitement—you read it right. If we are able to let go of our hyper awareness of what we think others are thinking of us, failure stops being a team sport to become an individual one. And what a complicated and exhausting sport it is: worrying about how we hypothesize others would interpret and then judge our actions is not for the weak. It requires some special talents: the ability to read minds, extrapolate feelings, and predict behavior—all in advance of things actually happening. Were we really half as good and accurate in such prognostications as our inner critical voices think we are, we would all be rich from winning the lottery. Multiple times. Plus, it also puts the other in a box: it prescribes them feelings and actions they have not yet taken—which makes them simple fixed beings in our mind and fails to give them the same latitude to be more complex and to change that we want for ourselves. Thinking that way, making up stories in our heads, is a race to the bottom: we feel judged and, in turn, we judge others—all before anyone does anything.

Instead, when we are able to and shift the energy we put into worrying (consciously or not) about what others will think of us toward actually doing what we think we should, we will find ourselves advancing faster in whichever area or effort we try. When all the distractions fall by the wayside, you may find yourself actually enjoying the challenge at hand and looking forward to the outcome. That is why people put puzzles together, build models, do crossword puzzles, play video games, run marathons, build businesses, write books... We engage in things we are going to enjoy and learn from even though we may not have all the particulars worked out when we first start. The excitement that sprouts from failing forward is the budding certainty that we are inching closer to the vision we first subscribed to, even if the picture on our minds is still fuzzy. This helps us advance toward the end goal we set for ourselves. Progress and movement along the road can keep us energized because we know we are making way. Failing fast and forward is how we make progress. Vygotsky and Dweck help us understand that learning process in greater detail so it can become easier for us to heed TS Eliot's advice to have the experience and not miss the meaning.

TIME TO CHOOSE: JERUSALEM OR DAMASCUS?

Hopefully, all the thinking and reflecting we have done have prepared us to make the decision we ultimately need to make: will we move forward, even though the path ahead may not be clear, or will we retreat to the comfort of what is known and perhaps wait for another day to reconsider change? In Paul's terms: shall we go back to Jerusalem or continue to Damascus?

Transferring the symbolism of Paul's journey to our own lives, we can see that we all have our own Jerusalem and our own Damascus. Jerusalem symbolizes everywhere we have been, everything we have done, everyone we have built relationships with, every habit we have developed. Damascus, on the other hand, stands for the new things we desire, the new relationships we wish for, the new places we want to go to, and the new habits we wish to build—regardless of whether they include people, places and things from the past in a new manifestation or not. Everything we have visited and experienced so far has had but one purpose: to build us up to make that choice. Do we retreat to Jerusalem or plow ahead to Damascus?

Jerusalem will always beckon us. The known, the familiar, the comfortable are powerful forces pulling us back. Like gravity, they act on us even when we are not aware: they are the places we always like visiting, the food we always like eating, the TV shows we always like watching, the work we always like doing, the thinking processes we always espouse, the people we always like spending time with... The list can be long. Our Jerusalem, in a way, is the habits and customs each one of us has created over time and that we carry within us. Jerusalem is concrete, palpable, and predictable. Because of that, it is also safe. It symbolizes our history, our story, our past and, many times, our identity. Letting go of our private Jerusalem is no easy feat.

Damascus will always whisper to us. The new, the untried, the potential of what can be are alluring possibilities inviting us forward. Like poetry, they entice us to a new place filled with the promise of new beauty. They represent the dreams we have, the changes we want to make, the goals we wish to achieve, the relief we want for ourselves or others, the new relationships we want to build, the difference we desire to see or make in the world... The wishlist is also long. The Damascus that we each have in our hearts and minds can be intangible or unpredictable. It stands for everything that can be: a new starting point, a new future, a new relationship, a new life and, possibly, a new self. Jumping to grasp the Damascus we carry in our hearts is no easy task.

Ultimately, however, the time comes to decide in

which direction we will trek. Will we go back to Jerusalem to stay within Vygotsky's innermost circle and perhaps satisfy ourselves with living in Dweck's fixed mindset? Or will we head over to Damascus, making the trip toward Vygotsky's outermost circle with Dweck's growth mindset strapped to our backs? Will we ignore the most knowledgeable other who calls us forward? Will we work in or shy away from our zone of proximal development? Will we go for the experiences even if we struggle with their immediate meaning, or will we deny them altogether?

If the choice seems extremely daunting, there is something else we should consider that could help us make it easier to move forward: this is not a mutually exclusive choice. We will not lose our Jerusalem forever if we choose Damascus, nor will we never be allowed to dream of Damascus again if we go back to Jerusalem. Choosing one over another in this moment of our lives does not mean we have completely written the other off—unless we want to do so. We can still visit. Those who have moved cities in their lifetime may comprehend this more easily: the experiences you have had go with you wherever you move. They remain with you as memories and as important building blocks of your identity. Choosing to go somewhere new is not necessarily a denial of all the places —or the person—we have been before. It simply is a statement of preference, of new direction. And it may not be forever either: after all, who is to say we will not move again?

With that in mind, the time has come to act. Which way shall we go? Shall we head back to Jerusalem or move forward to Damascus? Paul has made his choice. It is time we make ours.

WHAT WE LEARN FROM PAUL AND HIS DECISION TO GO AHEAD

The fifth lesson we take from Paul's journey to Damascus and the allegorical meaning it can hold for us is the awareness we will have to make—and commit to—key choices in our lives while we feel less than prepared to do so. We will have to choose between moving forward or returning back to the comfort of our status quo. By revisiting his story, we see that Paul had to make one of the most consequential choices of his existence exactly when he was at his most frail. Newly blind, confused, and emotionally alone after an unexpected event that turned his life upside down, he had to decide what was next for him: would he retreat back to the safety of his known world to find the comfort he knew or would he embrace the new path of self-discovery that presented itself to him in that moment? He chose to advance, to courageously move forward into uncharted territory, even while blind.

As we sit with Paul for a while, we know his choice was not an easy one—as ours are likely not to be, either. The world as it was called to him—as it does to us, every day. As we entertain all sorts of change, from the mundane to the monumental, from the imposed to the voluntary, we too will have to struggle with making decisions when we are not at our perceived best. Whether we are still shell-shocked by unexpected professional changes, still traumatized by the loss of people or opportunities, still feeling the aftershocks of relationships abruptly changing, or simply unsure about what really fills our buckets, we will have to choose how to handle the circumstances we have before us.

On top of the challenges of deciding, Paul's experience also teaches us we will have to account for the gravitational pull that our friends, family, and acquaintances exert on us. While they will likely point us back to Jerusalem, to the status quo they are understandably familiar with, we will have to make up our minds as to which way we will go. Changing—or not changing— because we sense that is what others want is not sustainable. And it should not be the principle that guides our lives, either. Just as a rocket needs enough fuel to break through the atmosphere into outer space, we will have to tap into the power of our convictions to shift into a new orbit. Comfort will never provide us with enough strength for new enterprises. Only the sheer power of our will and our convictions can take us there.

In examining Paul's difficult choice, we also learn to appreciate discomfort—not for the pain it may bring, but as the indicator it is. Discomfort, when well understood, becomes a reliable friend who points to the presence of an opportunity for growth. To further investigate the idea, we invite Lev Vygotsky to the table and see that the learning process requires a leap from our comfort zone to an area of discomfort (ZPD) where, with the help a more knowledgeable other (MKO), we do enough processing and struggling to allow the difficult task at hand to become familiar and comfortable. In that, we grow—and realize

that everything that is comfortable today was once uncomfortable before we mastered it.

We thus arrive at the realization that we have always
been creatures of expansion—we may have just forgotten
it. Our previous successes may have blinded us to the fact
that, before we succeeded at anything, we probably failed
many times. And that we may have to fail forward again
before we ascend to greater levels of achievement. Thus,
we slay the magical dragon of failure that lives in our
heads, rent-free; we transform it into the reliable page
who carries our shield and weapons and who helps us
train to become better knights during our personal quests.
Connecting the dots further, we understand we ought to
constantly remind ourselves that uncomfortable learning
processes will happen again, that we will need to stretch
beyond what is safe, easy, and comfortable to grow again.
We will always need a growth mindset if we are to
progress.

In doing so, we bring Carol Dweck back to our table to
rejoin our internal conversation with Paul, and sit her
right beside Vygotsky. Together they remind us—in stereo
and completing each other's sentences—of the importance
of trying new things and of refusing to be stuck in the
false idea that our abilities are fixed and immutable. T.S.
Eliot, sitting quietly, nods in agreement and poetically
chimes in that only those who risk going too far can
possibly find out how far one can go. That, they all agree,
is the only way to learn—the only way to have the experience and not miss its meaning. From that general consen-
sus, the conversation takes on a more lively energy as it
focuses not on the challenges of discomfort but on the

excitement of learning. Having better understood the mechanism of learning and being reminded that the price of achievement is temporary discomfort, we feel more comfortable silencing our conversation for a second and turning to Paul once more for wisdom...

Taking his time, Paul looks at each one of us with the tenderness of those who have walked the road before and know what lies ahead for us. He then then simply smiles as if to say: "Look at me: had I never made the decisions to go ahead, I would not be here today. I would still be Saul." Do you hear your future beckoning? Time to make your decision.

LESSON 6: THE UNEXPECTED HELP

The sixth lesson we learn from Paul and his journey is a welcome one: help always comes when we are committed to moving forward on our own road to Damascus. After we have spent much time and effort focusing on developing new awareness and undertaking tough inner changes to better navigate our pilgrimage, the news that the universe will come to our rescue is uplifting—and maybe even somewhat of a relief. But it will do so at the right time, at the wrong place, and in a manner that it is often unexpected. So much so that, unless we have new eyes with which to see, we might miss it altogether—or confuse it for something else.

Nonetheless, it is a great reminder that we are not alone even if it may feel like it at times. After a lot of introspection, doubt, and internal processing, it is only normal that we get used to facing inward and forget to look out and up. Especially when we are entangled in the web of challenges that lead to growth, it is easy to lose sight of the fact something greater than ourselves is keeping an eye on us at all times and nudging us forward when needed. This sixth lesson we learn from Paul's journey to Damascus comes at the right moment to remind us exactly of that—and that we are destined to progress, even when the odds may seem insurmountable. Prior to moving forward, let us revisit Paul's story to see what lessons we can glean from his experiences before we dive into how they can inform our own journeys.

PAUL'S STORY: THE UNEXPECTED HELP

After deciding to continue his journey despite his blindness, Paul finally arrives in Damascus. These past few days have been like nothing he has ever experienced before. He has had to re-evaluate everything he held certain under the sun. But he is here: Damascus. The voice told him to proceed to the city, and his heart agreed, so he did. He persevered through the desert, relying on his travel companion to see him through. He is tired and emotionally drained, but at least he has reached his destination.

In the city, he goes to those he knows for shelter. As a renowned political figure, Saul should have no problem finding a place to stay. After all, the prevailing custom mandates good hospitality, and for a respected member of the Sanhedrin such as himself, surely it will be no problem to find someone of good social station to host him. Most would even think of it as an honor. He will then be able to rest and recover while he waits for whatever comes next. He certainly could use a comfortable place to lay down his head and reflect.

Yet, door after door closes on his face. It seems none of his previous acquaintances are willing to receive him in their homes

*after he tells them of his meeting with the Christ and his new direc-
tion in life. His change is too much for them: they do not want to
risk their reputations by associating with someone who openly
favors a dead rabble-rouser from Nazareth. If word got out that
Saul was staying at their homes, it would be akin to political
suicide. His old circle of friends and connections all have aspirations and enjoy comforts they are not willing to sacrifice, so they
find excuses to decline. Saul may have had a place with them at any
time; Paul, on the other hand, is not welcomed in Saul's old circles.
Paul is on his own.*

*What will he do? Devoid of options and of clarity about what
is next, he and his traveling companion need a place to stay. But
what is left? No one he knows will receive him in their homes. He
feels truly alone: neither Jews nor the followers of Christ will have
him. His only option is to do something he would never have done
before: find a place for hire somewhere. They will have to find a
room in someone's home or rent spare space from a merchant. It
will be a departure from what he is used to. Neither will be guaranteed to be clean or safe. He has some money left; it could hold him
for a couple of days.*

*They find shelter and they wait. And wait. Paul's travel
companion, essential to getting him to Damascus, is also wavering;
he never did want to come to Damascus after Saul's fall from the
horse, but did so to ensure Saul's safety. Now, a day or two later, he
too is worried about being associated with this new Saul who is
outspoken about his experiences with the Christ. He too fears the
backlash of the established community and worries for his liveli-
hood. Sensing his concerns and understanding that this is his
journey and not his companion's, Paul releases him to return to
Jerusalem.* [1]

Paul continues to wait. Completely alone, having had his world turned upside-down by the very person he had hated the most, he finds himself in an unkempt spare room somewhere he would have never visited before all of this—somewhere unbecoming to the likes of Saul. He is blind and defenseless. He is unable to protect himself against the dangers of the world, especially on this side of the city. And he sits shrouded in doubt. He simply does not know where to go next. He knew to come to Damascus. From here, he has no idea where to go.

"For three days," the book of Acts tells us, "he was without sight, and neither ate nor drank"[2] as he struggled with his new reality. Paul has made the leap, has walked the rest of the desert blind, and arrived at Damascus. Now he has hit a wall he has no idea how to overcome. There is little else he feels he can do.

Unbeknownst to Saul, Jesus has also appeared to a man named Ananias, described by the book of Acts as a disciple who is also in Damascus.[3] After what must have been a very interesting conversation for Ananias—since he knows full well who Saul of Tarsus is and what he has done to followers of the Christ—he agrees to go meet Saul at the inn. There, Ananias lays hands on Saul and tells him he has been sent to heal his sight. "Immediately something like scales fell from his eyes, and he regained his sight."[4] Everything changes.

When Paul was at his lowest, after he had done everything he thought was right to grow and change for the better, the Universe threw him a lifesaver. He could see again because of the kindness of the most unlikely of strangers and, better yet, had met the first person who would accept and support this new version of him. The unexpected help came when he needed it the most —and thus Saul was finally reborn into Paul.

OUR LESSONS: THE RIGHT TIME, THE WRONG PLACE, AND THE UNEXPECTED MESSENGER

This part of the story also brings us good news: not all of our journey is uphill. Some parts of our own road to Damascus slope down to help us catch our breath and push us forward to continue our walk. Such moments are a very welcome reprieve from the long and arduous climb we all face in our lives. They come just at the right time, when the legs under us start to falter and we begin to think of stopping the journey altogether. They can also come when we are in the wrong place, when we have led ourselves to a state of mind that is not conducive to growth and cannot see a way out of it. Finally, they may also come in unexpected ways. Despite all of it, they always come. Help always comes. For everybody. The question that remains is whether we will have the presence of mind to recognize the help and the fortitude to leverage it.

THE RIGHT TIME

For help to be most effective, it must come at the most appropriate time. Timing is everything. If it arrives too soon, we may not recognize it or accept it because we may think we have everything under control. Arrive too late and, well, it is too late for us to leverage it. There is an analogy to baking somewhere in there: take your cake out of the oven too early and it is not ready. (You may have to put it back in.) Leave your cake in for too long, and it may not be a cake anymore. Neither option will do your stomach good. On the other hand, get it right and you have something to behold—not only for yourself but for others as well. (Cake-eating should always be a communal sport.)

One of the tricks to successful baking outcomes, it seems, is impeccable timing. As it turns out, God appears to be an incredible baker. The universe keeps showing up for us at exactly the time when we need help the most. Let's take Saul, for example: had Ananias showed up to meet him at the gate into Damascus, would Saul have learned to be comfortable with his new self on his own? Saul would have simply been handed over from one companion to another—from his travel companion to his new Christian companion. Instead, Saul had to spend some time by himself, brewing and distilling his experiences and thoughts in the crucible of solitude before he could produce something the world could drink. Such experience certainly served him well. Through it, he learned at least one powerful lesson: what it is to truly feel alone in the world.

Up to that point, Saul's life had been relatively devoid of challenges. Born to a family of privilege, young Saul received a great education and enjoyed one of the greatest benefits of his time: Roman citizenship. Athletic and intelligent, it did not take too long for young Saul to experience success. At a young age, he made a splash in the rabbinical world and quickly climbed the religious ladder. Soon enough, Saul enjoyed considerable fame within Jewish circles, to the point of receiving the now-dubious honor of persecuting and executing Stephen, the first martyr of Christianity. Eventually, he would receive a seat on the Sanhedrin, the greatest body of Jewish law at the time. By all accounts, Saul experienced a meteoric rise. It is highly probable that, had Saul been your son, you would have been extremely proud of his accomplishments.

Yet, while he remained steadfastly committed to the idea of God and justice, young Saul had never really experienced serious hardship. So much so that, one could argue, the young man, so zealous about the word of God within his community, lacked the empathy to comprehend many of the people who looked to him for spiritual guidance. For Saul, religion was about leadership and discipline; it was about skill, status, and authority. Compassion and kindness were not on his radar—they were things that only emerged later, with Paul. It is not a stretch of the imagination to say that the period of deep isolation and forlornness Saul experienced while blind in Damascus was instrumental in forging a new understanding of human emotions for Paul. An understanding which would prove foundational for the work he was to carry out in the coming decades, when he traveled the world consoling people and pointing them to hope and to a better life to come.

Had Saul not fully internalized the lesson of solitude and anguish offered by the experience of being left newly blind and lonely in someone's spare room waiting for something to happen, would we even have a Paul? Had he been rescued earlier from his blindness while he still had helpful companions next to him, would Saul have developed the depth of understanding of the human condition that allowed him to be such a sought-after counsel? We may never really know. Yet, what we do know of Saul before he became Paul would make him an unlikely candidate to be the author of incredibly poetic passages such as the one in his first letter to the Christian community in Corinth,[5] where he extols the virtues of love. This most often-quoted passage in Christian weddings everywhere tells us that love is everything a young, brash Saul was not: patient, kind, not proud, not self-seeking, trustful, hopeful...

In short, Saul needed to bake in the oven of his own afflictions for a while before life would use someone else to pull him out. Taking Saul out of the crucible of solitude too quickly would have hindered his ability to become the Paul we know. That little room in Judas's[6] home (a different Judas, mind you) acted as Paul's own oven: it may have been different, uncomfortable, hot, and extremely unpleasant. Yet, it was exactly what he needed. And Paul was pulled out by destiny at the right time.

THE WRONG PLACE

Paradoxically, what Saul would have considered to be the wrong place to stay in Damascus was exactly the right one. That room was far from what Saul would have been used to and much less than we would have hoped for. Like all of us, Saul was sometimes a prisoner of his own expectations. And if we give them too much power, expectations can become silent tricksters. Whether they are high or low, good or bad, conventional or idiosyncratic, expectations draw us into a fixed frame of mind that generally leads to frustration. Simply put, when things don't develop as we expect, we get frustrated. A product of our egos, expectations unconsciously trick us into believing the world should be a certain way—the way we think it should be. *Our* way.

Furthermore, expectations have an added danger to them: they can calcify our habits over time. When we keep meeting our own expectations of what is to happen and how, we keep believing that is the way the world works—and that nothing needs to change. They are also insidious: do something enough times a certain way and you get used to it—regardless of whether it is a potentially "good" or "bad" thing. They help build in us a false sense of permanence and security. In a way, expectations are close cousins to habits: they may not live under the same roof but are acquainted with each other well enough to come in and out of each other's houses pretty frequently.

All that is to say: expectations can cement us into certain habits of thinking that are hard to break free from. And, when we are on our way to doing different things—or doing things differently—we need to change our thinking habits. So sometimes life takes us from our places of comfort, the "right places," and puts us in much different ones—the "wrong ones," so to speak. It just turns out the wrong places are just right to break our old expectations and habits and to teach us how to see anew.

That is exactly what happened to Saul: removed from his places of comfort, he had to calm his inner storm while somewhere unfamiliar. Instead of Jerusalem, the city he lived in, it was Damascus. Instead of the places he knew, it was a location he had never seen before. Instead of the people he was familiar with, it was no one. Everything was different—and that was the catalyst to change he needed at the (right) time. While in this different geographic place, Saul was able to go to a different *mental* place. Because he had nothing familiar going on at that moment, Saul was forced to reach out for something new and outside of his usual repertoire. He did. And he found it. He found new, solid ground under his feet—but only because he leapt. And Saul only had to leap because where he found himself was not where he was used to being or wanted to be.

Looping back to us, the parallels are not too hard to make. Every so often we will be so entrenched in our ways that life will need to remove us from where we are and put us in the "wrong place." This "nudge" may not be pleasant, but it is effective. Sometimes it is only when we find ourselves in completely unfamiliar circumstances that we are required to change the way we think or act. But let us go beyond the physical and into the emotional and the spiritual, for that is what ultimately really matters. A change of physical scenery can help speed up our inner transformation, but it is not a goal in itself. The goal is the transformation of our mental outlook. It just so happens that a change in physical location sometimes helps us see things differently.

As a matter of fact, the whole tourism industry has been built on that concept: go somewhere different and feel different. Vacation somewhere exotic and feel alive. Visit Paris for romance. Go to London for culture and tradition. Travel to Greece or Italy for history. Safari in Kenya for adventure. Et cetera. While you may find romance in Paris, culture in London, history in Greece and Italy, and adventure in Kenya, hopefully we can all agree they are present elsewhere too. We have just accepted specific frames of minds and, in doing so, we live them as our reality. But what is preventing us from finding romance in Germany, culture in India, art in New Zealand, and history in Brazil? The point here is not to vilify travel industry marketing but to highlight that a change of scene is one thing that can contribute to a change in mental attitude. And that we are in charge of how we see the world—and where we "travel" to mentally.

With that perspective in mind and with Saul's example in heart, the "wrong places" can begin to look very different for us. If before they seemed to be places of pain or even punishment, this mindset sees them as catalysts for transformation. That job loss that deprived us of daily experiences with our coworkers, the departure from our longtime home due to the end of a long relationship; the move to a different city for a new job—all were key moments that teed us up for new learning. They may not have been pleasant at the time but, in retrospect, they may have seeded the beginning of new adventures, accomplishments, or phases in our lives. Maybe when the universe puts us under stress and we begin to crack under the pressure, it is not to make us crumble but to let some new light in.

The true question that remains is whether we have already developed the skills and awareness to understand that hardships are inflection points in our lives. They may be filled with discomfort and even pain, but they are also ripe with possibilities. By exercising our mental muscles and constantly reminding ourselves of this larger perspective, we take significant steps toward becoming proficient in understanding why we find ourselves in this seemingly wrong place. And if we are able to do so while the uncomfortable experience is still happening, we can chip away on the anxiety and fear they tend to elicit. Doing so makes the journey easier.

Ultimately, the choice about how we see where we are is ours—and therein lies much of the magic. Do we choose to see it as a place of gloom and doom, or do we opt to view it as a catapult for growth, ready to launch us into the next stage of our lives? Interestingly, the world will remain the same, but our inner reality can be fundamentally transformed. All it takes is a new perspective—and sometimes the wrong place at the right time.

THE UNEXPECTED MESSENGER

If popular wisdom is correct about good things coming in threes, then we need one more important component to complete our lesson: *the unexpected messenger*. So far, we have investigated the *when* and the *where*. Now we jump into the *whom*. As in: who else may be involved in getting us the help we need? After all, God helps people through people—so everyone can grow. More specifically, we turn our gaze to Ananias, the unexpected messenger who came to Paul and helped him see again.

That Ananias is the one who comes to Paul's rescue, in that unassuming backroom somewhere in Damascus, should not go unnoticed. It is almost a textbook case of dramatic irony. Ananias, an early exponent of Christianity, was one of the very people Saul was targeting in his trip to Damascus. After all, Saul's mandate was to find any followers of the prophet of Nazareth, man or woman, and bring them bound back to Jerusalem[7]. Not exactly a task one takes on halfheartedly. Thus, we would not be exaggerating if we said that Saul was helped by the very thing he persecuted. Let that sink in for a second and marvel at the universe's sense of irony—and its symbolic implications.

Sometimes, the things we least expect are the ones which surprise us the most. We are so trapped in our preconceived notions, our pre-built construct of the world, that we do not expect to be rattled in that manner. When we are, it really hits us. Take Saul again: the very thing he sought to exterminate was what helped him when he needed it most. It was Ananias who helped him regain his eyesight. In essence, that which Saul hated the most was what made him see the world anew. This lesson should not be lost in the wind: that which pushes us to the edge, that which elicits the greatest emotional responses from us, that is what can be our greatest teacher. Vygotsky had talked to us about discomfort in learning, but sometimes we think of discomfort only in its mild manifestations. Sometimes we forget that big pain and frustration are also uncomfortable. More than that, they are formidable drivers of progress. Whether it is anger, hate, deep aversion, desolation, depression, or anything else, it behooves us to try to understand what lesson they bring with them about the way we are living and thinking about the world.

Unless we enjoy large helpings of humble pie, whatever "pushes our buttons"—what bothers us, sticks in our craw, gets under our skin—should warrant greater attention and scrutiny from us. If we have developed some sort of emotional response, it is because we have established some form of emotional connection. If something is not important to us, it does not register on our radars. We are just indifferent to it. If it does register, it is because it matters to us—good or bad, consciously or unconsciously. Therefore, we should stop and make time to learn about these things—even the ones we are not fond of. Especially the ones we are not fond of. Reflection has to happen for learning to take place. It either comes on our terms when we make time for it, or it happens forcefully, when life sends us unexpected messengers to show us the way. Paul's case falls in the latter category.

Had Paul been less arrogant from the beginning toward the new way of thinking about religion and spirituality that the Christ brought forth, he would not have needed to face such a steep learning curve. Had he been more open, more flexible, he would not have needed to eat such a large slice of humble pie all at once. Imagine how hard it was to go through all the challenges he went through and to finally be helped by Ananias, a symbol of the very thing he detested to begin with. At that point, he already knew he had to change his ways—Ananias standing before him was not a subtle message, but a clear reminder of how off he had originally been. A final slap in the face, if you will.

Sometimes that piece of humble pie is really hard to swallow. And since coffee goes well with pie, consider this: when "brewing" life, it may be more palatable to drip your challenges a little at a time into your daily cup than to have it flooded with everything at once. That way you can at least sip it at your own pace instead of having to gulp it all down before it overflows. Reflecting early and often saves us from having to drink it all at once.

But let's push coffee and pie aside for a second. Ananias was not just something that happened to Paul. The unexpected messenger visits all of us—it just comes dressed differently, according to our own experiences, needs, and circumstances. Chances are we can draw a line or two to our own lives. What are the things that have irked us to the point of avoidance? What are the tasks or projects we have been putting off because they were not pleasant? What are some of the events or people who rub us the wrong way? What are the things we disdain or are arrogant about? No matter the answer, one important follow-up question can make all the difference: why is that the case? Let's, sit down, buckle up, and have a hard conversation with ourselves. We would do well to sit with these questions now and again and eat our pie and drink our coffee at our own pace before we are rushed by life to do so later.

Something else pretty spectacular also happens when we learn to see the world anew: the things we look at change. Yes, we do learn to look at new, different things during our journey. But we also learn to look at the old things differently. As if by magic, the messenger itself can change shape before our eyes. If before the messenger was something we disliked, feared, or avoided, it now becomes a welcomed and valued teacher—but only when we have new eyes with which to see. Ananias, whom Paul persecuted, was the same person who introduced him to the nascent Christian community in Damascus and got Saul on his way to becoming the Paul we know. Our messengers are likely to do the same: besides removing the scales from our eyes so we can think differently, they are also going to open doors to new realities and introduce us to new avenues of action.

If all of this seems implausible, just look to your past and you may find you have already been visited by an unexpected messenger: perhaps it was the end of a relationship you were not ready to let go of, maybe it was a health problem that crept up on you unexpectedly, or maybe it was a change in your professional life you did not see coming. The messenger came for you, so you will be the one to best identify it. Regardless of how it showed up in your journey, you may now be able to understand how it changed your life and taught you new things. Do not be surprised if you now find yourself grateful that those difficult things happened in the first place—because they have led you in new directions you would not have otherwise gone. To think that way is not a sign of masochism—just an indication of your growing self-awareness.

And like that Ananias is transformed from foe to friend. As Saul metamorphoses into Paul, we can see how his perception of Ananias also changed. For Saul, Ananias was someone to be apprehended, shackled, and eliminated. For Paul, Ananias was a welcome blessing who relieved some of his suffering and served as a shoulder to lean on during a time of great need. In fact, we can only imagine the special place Ananias may have occupied in Paul's heart: if you were Paul, would you forget Ananias easily? Yet, Ananias himself had not changed. Paul's perception of the world had changed significantly, but Ananias remained Ananias. That is to say: when we change the way we look at things, the things we look at change. It is, literally, a matter of perspective—one we create and control through the incredible power of our minds and perceptions.

That, in itself, is a powerful lesson: we get to dress our messengers in whichever garb we would like. If we opt to consider them the villains of our story who bring pain and injustice into our lives, they will be that. If we chose to see them as teachers who have come to guide us in growing and becoming better, they will be that. However we see them, that is who they will be for us. Ananias will be who Ananias is. Yet for Saul he was the enemy while for Paul he was the healer; from Saul, he drew out hatred and anger, and from Paul he elicited gratitude. These are vastly different perspectives which bring with them vastly different emotional charges. Which of those do we want in our lives? Taking a step further, we should consider that how we see our challenges gives us clues as to how we understand ourselves in life: are we the victims of the world's unfairness or the agents of our own growth and happiness? The choice is, no doubt, entirely ours. Which Ananias do we want in our lives?

WE ALL NEED HELP

There is also another important truth staring us in the face. Regardless of when, where, how, and who helps us, the irrefutable truth before us is that we all need it. At some point in our lives, we will need help. In fact, we need it every single day. Yet the idea of asking for help or receiving help is very difficult for many of us. Somewhere along the road, we let our insecurities get a hold of our minds, and we started to believe that receiving or asking for help is a sign of weakness. Nothing could be farther from the truth. Knowing one's own limits, seeking out help, and being open to growing are incredible traits that display emotional maturity and intellectual self-awareness. (In fact, these are characteristics every modern hiring manager is seeking when looking to add to their team: self-awareness, resourcefulness, and coachability. After all, would you hire an inflexible know-it-all to join your team? Probably not. So why be one?)

It is exactly because no one knows it all that we should make it clear to ourselves we all have something to learn. All of us. That's why we are all on our own journeys to Damascus. Along the way, we will stumble, trip, and fall. Many times. No exceptions. But we will also get up and continue the journey and we will be OK. As we have explored before, struggling is part of learning. Maybe that is why the Swiss-American psychiatrist Elizabeth Kubler-Ross once said, "I'm not OK, you're not OK, and that's OK." All of us are struggling with something, fighting some sort of internal battle no one else can see. Our learning process requires us to get our hands dirty with the clay of our own sculpture as we re-mold ourselves. But we should be OK with others assisting too: sometimes they have a better vantage point on our sculptures; sometimes they are more skilled at a particular technique than we are and can add to our work. We also do the same, assisting others in the crafting of themselves, and in the process we create an endless and beautiful pay-it-forward chain of events. There is no reason to avoid receiving or asking for real, honest help other than ego.

Again, let's go back to Paul. It took considerable outside help for Saul to become Paul: first Jesus appeared to him, then his travel companions escorted him to Damascus and helped him find a place to stay while he was blind, and, finally, Ananias helped him see again. None of these things would have happened if Saul insisted on acting alone. And it all happened in part because Paul took the help that was offered. We should too. It will make us better and, in turn, will help us make others better.

It is time we realize interdependency is a fact of life. No one goes the distance alone. Or as the metaphysical British poet John Donne would put it almost four hundred years ago[8], no one man (or woman) is an island entirely unto themselves. That we are interconnected and rely on each other is a testament to the beauty of the invisible fabric of life. It is the most efficient system one can design, where we can maximize individual strengths while building up our emerging abilities—all at the same time. It is a self-improving system created to always evolve and advance—the clear product of an incredible mind fully vested in our personal improvement. The physical and moral laws of the Universe are something to behold—and to keep in mind when we find ourselves downtrodden.

To sum things up: even if we must always make our own decisions by ourselves, we should not forget we are all interdependent and interconnected and, thus, can always count on receiving help when we are committed to our self-improvement. Paul regained his sight through the kindness of others. In turn and in time, he helped thousands of others see better too. All of that to say: give yourself some grace if you are struggling with accepting help. Embrace it and move forward.

THE DIVINE RADAR

There is something else in Paul's story that should strike a cord of hope and solace in our hearts: how Ananias finds Paul in Damascus. The Book of Acts tells us that Jesus appears to Ananias and tells him to go to Paul, as well as where to find him—that's part of the story. What we sometimes fail to keep close to our hearts is how Jesus knew where to find Saul in the first place. To know where to find Saul, he must have been following his steps. Symbolically, there is a lot in there that can speak to our hearts. In other words: Jesus had to be following Saul's progress to know exactly where to find him. And Saul, at that point, was not yet Paul—so it was not because of any special goodness or merit that Saul got help. It was just because Saul was. Just like we are. It was not a favor or mark of preference for Saul; it was just that the Creator watches over all of us, regardless of our perceived worth or stage of development.

The divine radar is always on, for all of us. The universe always knows where we are and is ready to spring into action and send us help when we truly need it, are ready for it, and can use it. Help always comes: at the right times, in the wrong places, and through unexpected means. It does not give us leeway to be reckless or imprudent with our lives, however; it just reminds us we are never truly alone and are cared for in ways that exceed our current understanding. Yet another reason for us to tread forward with confidence on our journeys to Damascus.

WHAT WE LEARN FROM PAUL AND THE UNEXPECTED HELP HE GETS ALONG THE WAY

The sixth aspect of Paul's journey to Damascus we investigate together brings us a sense of renewed hope and optimism: we always get help when we are on our road to self-betterment. It is a welcome breath of fresh air after we have done so much soul-searching and internal work. Help may happen differently than how we would expect or want it to, yet it happens. As we develop a new way of looking at life and the world around us, it becomes easier to spot it—and to embrace it.

Realizing help is always present can be an incredible moment of awareness for all of us: that even when we are downtrodden, when we are hurt and feeling blue, when we feel like we've been abandoned, have lost our sight, have nothing to our names, and are forgotten in a corner of the world that is not ours, God is with us. Help always comes at the right time, when we are in the wrong places, and through unexpected means. For Paul, it came when he was blind and alone, when he was by himself in the back room of someone else's home in a less-than-luxurious place in a city that was not his own, when he did not know what else to do—and it manifested through the most unlikely of messengers: Ananias. For us, it will take place in different ways. Whether it is by shaking us up in the realm of personal relationships, health, faith, career, ideology, or in any other area you can think of, life always intervenes before we dig our heels in too deeply into our own unhealthy ways and do more damage to ourselves than we are allowed to.

It is the unexpectedness of it all that is sometimes needed to break us out of our established thinking processes, to shed mental habits that will not help us in the next phase of our existence—even if they have served us well in the past. In order to undertake change, we must be open to it. And to crack us open for change, life sometimes has to place us in difficult situations to help us break out of our calcified mindset. Without that impact, we may not pay attention. As it happens, we may feel totally out of control and think we are in the wrong place and that nothing makes sense—that we are flying blind. But this is necessary for better things to come; it allows us to surrender our old ways in anticipation of building better ones. It is how we make space for the new.

For as long as we fail to understand the purpose of the challenges before us, we will continue to struggle. When we understand the process, however, everything changes: we no longer see the difficult spots we go through in life as the wrong places, but the right ones for change; we no longer face the harsh moments of our lives as obstacles to crush us, but as catalysts for reinvention; and we no longer see the unexpected as pointless chaos, but as a wake-up call form the Universe that signals a higher order is realigning our path so we can grow and thrive. The unexpected messenger, those surprises in our lives that leave us aghast, come when we have stopped stretching our intellectual, emotional, and moral limbs and have become inflexible and sedentary. When we least expect, that which we least expect may have us thinking in the ways we would have least expected. And that is exactly what is needed—and that understanding sets us free.

Would we change if not exposed to the unexpected messenger? Perhaps eventually—but it would happen at a much slower pace. Would Saul have become Paul without Christ unexpectedly showing up on the road to Damascus and Ananias surprising him in the city? Would we be who we are today had we not faced the challenges that lie behind us? How, then, can we be what we ultimately must be—something greater and happier than what we are now—if we do not embrace the unexpected messenger? It will come at the right time, when we are in the wrong place in our lives, and it will manifest in unexpected ways—and all of that will be for our own good, because we are watched over and guided by something infinitely greater and more loving than we can ever imagine: God. So we continue on our journeys toward Damascus with the wind at our backs, a spring in our steps, and the certainty we are pointed the right way.

LESSON 7: A DIFFERENT DAMASCUS

Our seventh lesson from Paul's journey is not about the trek itself, but about Damascus—the destination. The city begs some consideration. When we look closer, Damascus takes on a life of its own and becomes a character in our story—one that goes almost unnoticed while it changes before our eyes. After all, the Damascus that Saul envisioned visiting was significantly different than the one in which Paul ultimately arrived. Yet, the city remained fundamentally the same. In this paradox lies an important reminder to all of us travelers: where we expect we will end up is not always exactly where we do. And that is not necessarily a bad thing. It says a lot about our goals, our expectations, and how they can change through time—and how we do too.

The journey we think will lead us to what we seek also has the power to change what we want. In that, it reminds us of the always flowing river of personal development within every one of us. We are always in flux. So far, we have considered the important changes that can take place while we are on the road. Now we turn our attention to the slow and unanticipated shift that can happen to what is at the end of the journey. It is only fitting that, as we prepare ourselves to walk our own roads, our final point of consideration is our destination. So we lift our eyes up from our feet, stretch our gaze into the distance and think of what is to come. To help us, we invite Paul to join us one last time.

PAUL'S STORY: A DIFFERENT DAMASCUS

As Saul sits in that small room on Straight Street waiting for something to happen, he cannot help but think of how much the world has changed in just a matter of days. Just a week or so ago, he assumed he would cross the gates of Damascus as a defender of the faith, a man of power and political stature in control of his own destiny and on his way to do great things persecuting all the misguided followers of this emerging cult he figured Christianity to be. As it turned out, he arrived not as the champion of the Sanhedrin but, instead, as a wandering blind man with little to his name and no friends to take him in. This was not what he had imagined. This was not the Damascus he expected. This was not what he had wanted. So he sits and waits. And he hopes. There is nothing else he can really do at this point. He cannot go back to what was before. He has changed.

———

YEARS HAVE PASSED since his encounter with Christ on the road to Damascus, and Paul marvels at how much things have changed. He is altogether a different person, transformed by the many experiences he has lived through since then. As he digs back into his memories, they almost seem foreign to him, distant echoes of a different person, a different life lived in a different time and place. He certainly faced other difficult situations during his travels since, but how much he learned in Damascus! What he thought was just a stop along his way to a greater role in the world turned out to be just that—but in a completely different way than expected. When he sought to collect outward accolades with which to build a prosperous future, Damascus taught him to leave them behind; when he hoped to make a bigger name for himself as the defender of the people, Damascus showed him how to let go of that ambition so he could actually become one; when he expected to shine and have the world recognize his brilliance, Damascus had him dim his own light and sent him back inside to rekindle it and start again.

Now he finds himself in a prison in Rome at the end of his life in similar circumstances: at the mercy of others and waiting for what is next. Yet the power of those convictions that started in Damascus all those years ago brought him here not by force, but by choice. How his world has changed! He once evaded it but now has chosen it... He stands fundamentally transformed: his life shifted from a focus on the ways of the world to an emphasis on the gifts of the spirit, from worrying about the outside to focusing on the inside. He looks back in time and feels immense gratitude for all that he learned years ago and everything that followed. The city that was to be just a stop in his life turned out to be a significant milestone, a new beginning. Damascus helped him transform himself in ways he had never expected and reach a level of personal fulfillment he could never have imagined. He will be forever grateful for all of it, no matter what is next.

OUR LESSONS: THE SHIFTING SELF AND ITS GOALS

The final gift Paul leaves us with is that of ongoing transformation and ever-growing perspective. It is one that can change the idea of change ever so subtly, from a means to an end to an end in itself. When we gain higher perspective and apply it to ourselves, the concept of change grows too. It shifts its nature from short-term to long-term and from temporary to ongoing. To get there, however, we need to have done the necessary inner work through our journey on the road. When we have, it is as if we graduate from a cursory to a more comprehensive understanding of the world and our role in it. The world seems deeper and more beautiful, more colorful, more purposeful, and more accepting.

Most of the time, we attempt change in or around ourselves to reach a goal we truly desire or that we have been unable to attain. Normally, change is just a vehicle for something. We recognize we need to do things differently to get there, so we open ourselves to trying new things and set ourselves in motion to achieve it. Sometimes, however, we may notice that such goals seem to lose their sparkle with time as we work toward them. Maybe they no longer have that allure for us. Perhaps they begin to feel less relevant. Sometimes, we may even puzzle over why we pursued them in the first place. Whatever the reason, the promise of achieving something you decided was important to you fizzles. You may have experienced that a couple of times in your life: perhaps you wanted to be a professional sports player, a famous artist, or a firefighter when you were young. As you grew up, your interests shifted—and so did your goals. But this is not just a child's experience: everyday throughout the world we see people changing their perspectives about what they want for themselves and others. We are no strangers to it either: we change our minds about what our "dream" car, our "dream" home, and our "dream" job are; we revise relationship goals; we rethink a series of things and aspects of our lives that, all of a sudden, seem too small or too large for us. We do so not because they were not good enough to begin with—they were, based on what we knew and wanted at that point in time. But something changed and they no longer hold sway over our fancy. It is not necessarily about quality, sometimes it is just about interest. But what changed? We did.

STEP INTO THE RIVER

You cannot step into the same river twice—or so Heraclitus would have us believe. Heraclitus of Ephesus was a pre-Socratic Greek philosopher who lived in the 6th century BCE in what is now Turkey. We know little about him, and what we do know comes to us as short fragments attributed to him by later authors. Although he seemed to be unpopular during his time and was later scorned by some biographers, he did leave us with this rich and poetic image—one we could use as a metaphor for life as well as for ourselves. Plato later took that idea to mean that things are constantly in flux, regardless of how we perceive them.

As we take our shoes and socks off to step into Heraclitus's river, we wonder if there is something in this image that resonates with our experiences. Whether we think of the river as life or as ourselves, one thing seems true: things are constantly flowing by us and within us. At any moment in time, the river is exactly what it is. Right after, in the next moment, it changes: waters flow, ripples and currents form differently, small waves break at different places—without ever losing its greater identity, without ever ceasing to be a river. So does life, so do we— and so did Damascus for Paul. *What* it objectively was remained the same. *How* it was changed. We too remain the same people as we progress through life, but how we do so changes. Paul experienced a disconnect between the Damascus he expected and the one he experienced. Sometimes we too experience a dissonance between what we want at one phase of our lives and what we want at another. It could be that we achieved what we wanted and it was not as we expected, or maybe we just did not want to go there anymore—either way, things changed. Life may change, but it still is our life. The constant here is change. Such is the pattern of the universe.

INNER SHIFT

If it is indeed the case that constant change is in the universe's DNA, then we should see that reflected in many places. As the 18th-century French educator and philosopher Allan Kardec posited following the principles of the scientific method,[1] we can verify that something is true if it is repeated in different settings. One person can be mistaken or even deceived, but it is harder for multiple people to be so, especially if they are scattered in different places and different times. It is a guarantee for us all that something really is true. And if we see a pattern that holds true in different places, things, and times, it is also an assurance that there is a greater order to things—a proof of the existence of God, if you will. We leave that part for another time, however.

We see constant change everywhere: from the larger celestial bodies to the smallest cells in living things. That planets, stars, and galaxies are always moving, we already know. What we forget to internalize is that even our bodies are in constant flux. Yes, we are talking about the aging process, of course, but that sometimes seems somewhat abstract. We can (and should) go deeper than wrinkles and the unforgiving effects of gravity, which is what most of us often think of when we think of old age. But there is more: what we may sometimes fail to consider is the extent to and speed at which our bodies undergo incredible change every day at the cellular level. How much so, you ask?

According to the latest estimates, your body is made up of about 37.2 trillion cells[2]—and with very few exceptions, our cells do not live as long as we do. As we rarely reduce size as we age (thanks, American diet...), this means that your cells are constantly copying themselves to ensure the biological functions that need to take place for you to continue to live go on. Interestingly, different cells have different lifespans,[3] ranging from a few days (stomach cells) to weeks (skin cells) to months (red blood cells) to years (fat and bone cells). (Interestingly, brain cells do not regenerate as we age—which also explains a lot...) In the cauldron of chemical and biological activity that is you, all these things are happening at the same time, on different schedules, and in perfect coordination. Always. It is, literally, a universe of biological bodies interacting and working together for one single purpose: to give you life for as long as it is possible.

Feeling special? You should: our physical bodies are marvels of engineering developed during a grueling 200,000-year process—3.5 billion years, really, when we consider that we are the result of all the evolution of life on earth. Through every one of the 2,239,056,000 seconds that make up the average 71-year human life span, our cells work hard to ensure we go on by copying themselves over and over before they die—all without ever asking for vacation or for a raise. With all this change taking place at the biological level every second of our lives, it seems ironic that we are at times so intent on *not* changing—and maybe a tad ungrateful too. If our bodies did not change, we would die *a lot* earlier than we do. We would not even come to be, as our bodies are the result of cell multiplication from the start. In short: physical life is not possible without change. Not changing only makes sense if we want to be rocks—and that would be dumb... You do not often find *that* listed as a life goal. Nature seems to be sending us a very simple message: change or perish.

MOVING GOAL POSTS

Things are always in flux. As much as we may hate it, life is doing us a favor by always moving the goalposts on us. We do not often think that way, because we are almost always held hostage by our short-term thinking. In those instances, it can certainly be very frustrating to constantly find oneself ready to kick the proverbial football over the goalposts for a victory, only to find out they have moved again. At the same time, we will need to find a new goal after we score, anyway. If we didn't, there would be no more challenge or feeling of achievement to it after a while. As much as we think we do not want new goals, eventually we change our minds. There's change raising its fickle head again...

So how can we shift our thinking from operating only on the immediate, short-term perspective? How can we remind ourselves that life is more than just one or two specific accomplishments, more than a couple of kicks over the goalposts, so we should really be looking at how we play the entire game? How can we shift our focus from *doing* to *being*? We are, after all, *human beings*, not *human doings*. Doing is that moment we step into the river, which can and will always be different. Being is the river itself, which may change course, ebb and flow, but will not cease to be. Both have movement and action to them. What changes is perception. What dictates our experience is how we choose to see things.

GUIDING PRINCIPLES VERSUS OBJECTIVES

In that manner, it turns out we can do ourselves a lot of favors by changing the way we choose to perceive the world. We dove deeper into the process when we explored our own blindness. Now we may want to find a way to better frame our goals so they do not seem as shifty and so we do not find ourselves frustrated along the road. One possible way of achieving that and bringing a bit more permanence into our lives is focusing on guiding principles rather than objectives. By doing so, we can do two things at once: we can reduce frustration in our lives while also training ourselves to take a higher perspective to things. Rather than focusing on achieving a thing in itself, we can orient ourselves to the purpose behind it.

It's common to conflate an underlying need with a specific path, goal, or object we think will fulfill it. For example, we may be focused on buying an expensive pair of shoes because we think that will mean having a shoe that is both functional and good-looking, or get attached to the idea of a particular romantic partner when what we really want is to find someone who will make us happy and add to our life, or set as a goal getting a specific job because we think it's the one path to fulfillment and recognition. But when we get these things or connect with these people, we may find we didn't get the underlying thing we were seeking after all. If we are not careful, we may find ourselves stuck in a vicious cycle where we keep going back to search for fulfillment we cannot find in things.

When we overfocus on specific objectives, that some-times means we ignore the purpose we attach to them. It leads us to focus on the material rather than on the emotional and spiritual. But if we focus on guiding princi-ples, we can find ways to fulfill those underlying needs-- even if that means altering our specific goals. A guiding principle approach trains us to refocus our minds from the chasing of the specific and shallow to the pursuit of the inspirational and more profound.

TOWARD HIGHER PURPOSE

Don't be surprised, therefore, if your walk toward your Damascus begins to transform not only you, but your goals as well. That is what experience does: it makes us into more skilled hikers. And more skilled hikers often see better paths to follow along the journey. If we stop to think about it, we may find that more experienced travelers already trend toward fulfilling underlying needs rather than pursuing specific objectives, even if they may not call it that. They tend to focus on building things rather than achieving them. We can also see that mirrored in the reflections of our elders: as they approach the end of their physical journeys, their advice is almost always related to dedicating oneself to fulfilling guiding principles and not specific objectives. They suggest we spend more time with our families and loved ones and that we focus less on social recognition and wealth—in other words, that we follow our hearts more than our pockets or our egos.

If you already find yourself pondering these issues, it may be an indication your shift to the guiding principles phase has begun. The road is calling you to focus on higher purposes. Your Damascus is changing. If the experiences of other travelers—such as Paul—offer any foresight into what lies ahead, then we can expect our hearts and minds will nudge us toward considerations about the greater good and other lofty ideals. We will find ourselves feeling an invisible itch, one that constantly asks for our attention to guiding principles that speak to our heart and ultimate fulfillment. Questions about our place in the universe may start to arise. Doubts about our purpose in this life will follow. And, with luck, we will also ponder the impact we may have in this world. It is a shift that takes us from a singular focus on the self to the desire to lift others.

Sometimes, without realizing, these musings will land us in "God" territory—even if we are not aware. After all, purpose, meaning, and impact are concepts that are directly related to divinity, because only divinity can give us a lasting anchor to which we can safely tether our thoughts, hopes, aspirations and, ultimately, our actions. Not the divinity sold by organized religion (as we mentioned before), but the true deep contemplation and relationship with the Creator each of us must arrive at on our own as we marvel about the journey and the universe around us.

The journey to Damascus, ultimately, leads us to the realm of higher thinking. It leads us to grapple with purpose and meaning, with the relationship between order and chaos, with life and beyond. It may start with goals and purposes related to our physical existence and success but, at some point, it evolves to issues of a more essential nature: our psychological, emotional, and spiritual essence. When we knock at that door and it opens to us, when we see the world through new eyes, the challenge becomes how to realign our physical experiences with our new spiritual values, how to live our best lives in a way that honors our noblest aspirations, how to leave behind that which we thought was important before but that no longer holds sway over us in the same fashion—in short, how to leave behind that old version of us that no longer fits our new worldview and move forward, as the man from Tarsus had to leave Saul behind before becoming Paul.

ENDS AND BEGINNINGS

On the long road, beginnings and ends start to blur. The horizon looming in the distance—the end of our field of vision—may give us the impression of finality. We look back and think that is where we started. We look forward and feel what we can see may be the end. But that is only true if we do not move, and move we must. When motion factors in, we see ends and beginnings are illusions based on perspective. If we move in any direction, beginnings and ends change—because our perspective changes. In a way, traveling is understanding that beginnings and ends are arbitrary; they are psychological constructs we choose to accept in our lives. When we are faced with a large obstacle or difficult circumstance in our lives, we tend to think of it as the end of something when, in fact, it can very well be understood as the beginning of something else. For Saul, reaching Damascus was the end of the road; for Paul, it was the beginning of the journey. Both are true. The only difference is choice of perception—of mindset, if you will. Which one do we choose? Are we on Team Saul or Team Paul?

Interestingly, we still have a tendency to mourn ends when we should celebrate beginnings. We fear loss more than we are grateful for opportunities. We are still so focused on the here and now that it is hard to lift our heads to gain new perspective and see the big picture. This awareness is a simple but impactful one: it helps us understand whether we are still focusing on the visible world (represented by Saul) or if we have begun to transition to an intentional emphasis on the invisible and spiritual, represented by Paul.

This curious phenomenon is so ingrained that it is even present where we least expect it. Take organized Christianity, for instance: there is so much emphasis on Christ-nailed-to-the-cross that it often overshadows the beauty of Christ-resurrected; there is so much talk of "fearing God" that it at times overshadows the idea of a loving relationship with the Creator; there is so much focus on pointing out what one should *not* do, that it is hard to remember the Christ was intent on bringing us the "good news" and pointing us toward joyful living. Right in front of our noses is organized religion's inability to move from *constraining rules* to *guiding principles* and from focusing on inadequate behaviors to modeling positive ones. Some churches have not yet made the journey to Damascus themselves, wherein we leave the judgmental approach of the Old Testament (Saul) behind in favor of the more loving and accepting approach of the New Testament (Paul). Of course, there are plenty of congregations and groups out there that have made the leap and are doing a tremendous job of helping people find their place in the world through love, service to others, and positive personal transformation. This is not a condemnation of organized religion as a whole, but a reminder that this kind of thinking is so pervasive that it happens in places we least expect to see it—and that it affects groups as well (which makes sense, considering groups are nothing more than collectives of individuals with specific thinking processes and habits). An attachment to this old way of thinking may be why organized religion's influence in the world is waning—and why more and more people are describing themselves as spiritual but not religious.[4]

But all is changing: a new generation is among us and more and more we are looking to new beginnings instead of to old endings. More and more our world—flawed, materialist, and pessimistic as it still may be—is leading us to a greater perspective through enhanced connection to each other. It too is finding its way, transforming before our very eyes—just more slowly than it is easy to notice during one lifetime.

The universe always gives us the tools we need before we need them—and these tools are already here. Technological developments mean we can connect to each other and people throughout the world in ways we could never before. The question that remains is when we will realize that we need to pick them up and use them differently than we have so far—when we will use our resources to connect rather than divide us, to collaborate rather than compete. Societies have always had unexpected messengers that have helped us refocus and rethink our ways. They are too numerous to list, but the study of history is often a stark reminder of that—and a call to action for a better future. The 2019-2020 coronavirus crisis, for example, may look like the end of an era, but it can also be seen as a catalyst to a new way of thinking about our own lives and those of others. In the middle of all of this, one question remains: how do we choose to see that which is in front of us? Do we see it as an end or as a beginning?

WHAT IS YOUR DAMASCUS?

All of these considerations point to one simple end: figuring out what your Damascus is. You have no doubt been on an incredible journey, experienced things no one else has, developed a unique collection of perspectives unlike that of anyone else, and struggled through your own set of personal speed bumps and obstacles along the way—all of which have led you to where you are right now. During this entire process, you may have been so intent on navigating the challenges presented to you that you did not have time to ponder your ultimate destination. Or perhaps you did, but found it elusive because it continued to change along the way. Either way, how you arrived here does not matter as much as where you want to go next. How you traveled here may have informed who you are today, but it need not limit who you can be tomorrow.

The beauty of it is that the Damascus that lies ahead for you is entirely yours and yours alone. It is exclusively for you—we all have our own Damascus. Even if it may seem like we all want the same Damascus, each one of us will weave a different picture of what it will look and feel like in our minds. If we do not—if we do not spend the time imagining and deciding at which Damascus we want to arrive—then we cannot truly complain about where we end up. Or, as Lewis Carroll's Cheshire Cat would remind us, if we do not know where we are going, any road will take us there.[5] We should not leave our happiness up to happenstance.

Even if we do know what we want for our ultimate destination, we still need to make peace with the fact it may change over time. And that is OK. Regardless, it remains vital that we ask ourselves what our Damascus is, for it will dictate which road we take.

So, as you leave your Jerusalem behind and take to the road in search of what can be, what is your Damascus?

WHAT WE LEARN FROM PAUL AND HIS DAMASCUS

Our final opportunity for reflection about Saul's journey to becoming Paul leads us to consider our ultimate destination, our own Damascus. In following Paul's travels, we think of our own. He ultimately arrives where he planned, but finds a very different place than he expected. His Damascus had changed. In truth, what had changed was not the place itself, but Paul's goals and expectations. Paradoxically, Damascus still is the same place, but because his mindset and spiritual views had changed, it held a vastly different meaning to his heart.

His experience also points to something else: the idea that the places we think we want to go might not be the places that we need to go. The mindset we start with, which we think is going to lead us to success and prosperity, might not be the one that truly leads us to happiness. It also shows us that life is in constant flux—and so are we. That it is perfectly normal for us to change our goals along the way. In fact, we should expect to do so as we gain experience and develop a broader worldview. Like a river, we can ebb and flow without ever ceasing to be who we are.

Paul's story reminds us that our lives can change greatly from one moment to the next—and that such changes happen not only to us but also in us. That, during the course of our journeys, we do not just change strategies to obtain what we wanted and could not do before, but we also transform ourselves along the way. With it, our goals also change. Moreover, this interesting goal-changing phenomenon is likely to actually happen multiple times in our lives. Although it can be frustrating to feel like the goalposts are moving on us, it is part of the natural pattern of the universe. When we begin to see life with new eyes, we start to choose to shift our approach to happiness from the achievement of specific goals to the fulfilling of guiding principles. Those ever-moving goalposts stop bothering us as much as they did before. Instead, our higher perspective leads us to see the changes as exciting opportunities for growth that keeps us sharp— and as ways to keep developing our skills so we can be more.

In this journey from doing to being, we begin to find our true nature, our true worth, and our true joy. We contend with bigger questions of purpose and impact in the world—which require us to change our previous goals and objectives. We understand that beginnings and endings are mere constructs we impose on ourselves, and that we possess the incredible ability to frame our experiences in ways that will either victimize and constrict us or empower us to continue to expand all that we are.

Ultimately, we realize that our Damascus is always changing—as it should. Damascus is not a final destination but another stop on the road to somewhere else— something that may also change with time. We too are always transforming physically, emotionally, intellectually, and spiritually, so why should not our goals and aspirations shift as we evolve? Why should not our targeted destination change? All that it takes to transform Damascus is our minds and our will. It happens every day whether we are conscious of it or not, because the river within never stops flowing and never stops changing. We can help ourselves by focusing on the higher guiding principles we choose for ourselves—and revisiting them frequently because there is more beyond Damascus.

It is true that the Damascus Saul sought ended up being a completely different city than the one Paul entered. Yet, neither Saul nor Paul would have wanted it any different—because when the incredible light from the Christ shines in our lives, it transforms everything for the better by inviting us to change ourselves in ways beyond our understanding and to ends beyond our greatest desires. But none of it is possible without our active acquiescence to and participation in the transformation process. It is we who decide how and when to do it. It is up to us to decide what our Damascus should be and how to get there. Thus, we ask again: What is your Damascus?

OUR ROAD TO DAMASCUS AND BEYOND

So we have walked with Paul on his journey to Damascus. We have grappled with some of the challenges he faced as he felt compelled to take on the dusty roads of an uncertain future in search of self-discovery. As silent companions to his walking, we have spent time reflecting about seven symbolic lessons from his story. All in all, we have covered a lot of ground. But we know there is more—and you may feel it too. Beyond his journey of transformation lies our own. Beyond his road to self-realization we see our road to Damascus. It stretches before our eyes. It beckons us.

So what is next?

Ahead of us is our own journey. It is the path we must make for ourselves as we weave together the strands of the tapestry of our lives, one by one, through our daily choices. Fortunately, we have Paul's Damascene experience to reflect on and take with us. Because of it, we no longer feel as alone or at the mercy of uncertainty and chaos. We have learned with Paul what we may encounter along the way. His challenges, toils, and achievements inform ours. They shed some light on the way ahead, illuminating our path enough that we have a better sense of where to step, even if our roads are altogether different. Paul's story echoes in history to remind us that the journey we are embarking on has been made before, is possible and, more importantly, is worth it.

As we breathe in and take stock of things, we see how Paul has helped us be better prepared for our own traveling. Along with a new outlook, we have also gained new insights about what we may face—and sometimes a better understanding of what we have already encountered. Through his example, we have learned seven key lessons we can take with us in our backpacks as we make our own trails.

LESSONS FROM THE ROAD

The first is that our journey is our story, not that of others. That, even if we find ourselves surrounded by people we care and love, they may not always be there for us. It is to be expected that we may lose people or their support along the way, as life is ever-changing. That is a fact of life we must get accustomed to. As such, we must prepare ourselves to make our own decisions on the way to our Damascus. But, on the other hand, if we learn that we can sometimes feel alone even if in a group—just as Saul did on that dusty desert road with his travel companions—we also understand that we do not really lose people unless we let ourselves think we do. The experiences we shared and the love we have for them endure for as long as we want—and, thus, so does their presence with us. We can always keep them with us, no matter where we (or they) are; geography matters less and less as time goes by. We can find solace in knowing that new relationships are coming, and that moments of solitude along the way to change will be worth it.

The second lesson we take with us is that the transformative moments in our lives are often brought about by difficulties. As we let that sink in, we begin to deprogram assumptions we may have held about change and personal betterment being struggle-free endeavors. We remember that even in fairy tales there is hardship, conflict, and pain before the happy ending we seek and expect. Just as Saul was brought down by a blinding light from his high horse onto the hard and dusty ground of the road to Damascus, so will we at some point in our lives be brought low by new information that changes everything we believed. Life sometimes engenders difficult situations for us so we may fall back onto ourselves—and onto a better path. In understanding the power of life to redirect us away from paths that will not benefit us in the long run (even if we do not see it at first), we realize that challenges are powerful allies on the road to self-betterment—that hardship is not punishment but an opportunity for course correction. We thus embrace these destabilizing meetings with destiny as starting points to something better, rather than the tragedies we first think them to be.

The third reflection Paul's story leads us to is whether we are ready to ask some courageous questions of ourselves. It is a reminder that true change always starts inside. Even if the whole universe is pointing toward a better direction for us, it is we who must choose to go that way. Very little progress can happen in our lives without our conscious acquiescence or intention. We are the ones who have to determine if we truly want to change, what that change will be, and whether we are prepared to leave behind what lies behind to make space for what is ahead. Much like Saul did, we too have to engage in deep contemplations about purpose, meaning, and direction—or risk remaining in psychological limbo. Will we remain trapped in the desire to do something new without ever committing to change? Without being clear with ourselves about what we truly want for our lives, we will remain stuck in the same cycle of experiences in which we find ourselves.

The fourth key understanding we arrive at is that deep personal transformation often brings about a certain temporary blindness about life. Committing to something new, embracing the different, trying new ways of doing and being—all are departures from what we used to do before. As such, we often feel uncertain about what lies ahead and how to proceed when we are in the middle of the storm of change. It may often feel like we have lost our sight, our familiar way of navigating the world. Yet, we learn with Paul, this state of confusion affords us the opportunity to retreat into ourselves and develop a new way of looking at and understanding the world around us. Through this new lens, we see confusion not as chaos, but as a period of reorganization. It is a necessary step in the recrafting of ourselves because being or doing different requires us to see things differently.

The fifth lesson we take from Paul's experience is that we must actively commit to change if we are to reinvent ourselves. We must choose to move forward even when mired in confusion and uncertain of what is next. Deciding to change is a great milestone, but moving on that decision is the ultimate litmus test. Making the decision to put one foot in front of the other and go is a key moment for us. It is exactly those moments that test our resolve and commitment to change, that tell us whether we are ready to transform ourselves because an innermost conviction has taken root in our hearts—or if we are merely seeking the complacency of comfort. Paul had to make the choice: would he go back to the comfort of Jerusalem or would he venture forth into the uncertainty of Damascus? We too will have to make such a decision.

The sixth takeaway from our journey to Damascus with Paul is a reassuring one: help always comes along the way. When we set ourselves in motion toward noble purposes, the universe always responds. Although help may not present itself in ways we expect or desire, it is always there. For Paul, it came through Ananias, one of the very people he was persecuting. For us, it will likely also manifest in unexpected ways. But, now that we have learned to see again, we will be able to spot it—and also recognize that, for it to come, a force greater than ourselves must have directed it to us. And it could only have directed it to us if it knew where we were—because it has been with us and following us all along. In many ways, it is the culmination of our own journey: to know we have unwavering and unconditional support to take on all challenges may re-energize us to persist in our quest for personal transformation—to the end. When we internalize that, our hearts become less weary, our legs less tired, and our spirits breathe a little easier.

The final lesson we take from Paul's trip through the desert is that destinations and goals shift during our lives. The Damascus Paul arrived at was radically different than the one he first envisioned and expected—yet it was the same place. We too may arrive where we wanted to go, only to find it does not elicit the satisfaction and joy we had anticipated. This underscores the importance of constantly re-evaluating our goals and purpose in life—and realigning our expectations and intentions to reach destinations that will not change and are not fleeting: the bettering of self through the constant development of virtues and positive habits. With experience, we tilt ever more heavily toward virtues over victories, skills over stuff, and happiness over having.

BEYOND THE ROAD

But, ultimately, arriving at the Damascus in front of us is not the end of our whole journey.

Reaching the destination we seek is, no doubt, an important milestone—and a necessary one. It should be cause for jubilation and commemoration. Yet, our larger journey will continue beyond this time and this place—and beyond the Damascus we seek right now.

Paul's journey did not end at Damascus either. In fact, his most productive and fulfilling years came after—when, through many new travels, he put into practice everything he learned on the road to Damascus. (Yours may too.) If we follow his story, we learn in the Epistle to the Gala-tians[1] that, after his incredible transformation from Saul to Paul, he went into the desert for a period of reflection before forging the way to become the Paul we know today. This may also happen to us: we too should plan on taking time to reflect, even after reaching our destination, to take stock of how we are changing before we embark on the next leg of our journey.

At the end of it all, however, we take with us the ever-growing certainty that the exploring is often more impor-tant than the destination—because the exploring is constant and the destination temporary. So Paul's real value-add to us is not showing us where to go—because no one can really do that for us—but giving us tools that can make our exploring easier and more effective as we decide where we go next. And where do we go next? You already know that answer: only your heart can tell...

No matter where our hearts, minds, and feet take us next, however, a certainty that starts to permeate our souls the more we walk is that we are never truly alone in the journey. As we reflect upon our travels on the road and all the challenges we face and overcome along the way, it is sometimes easy to forget that it was a brief moment of light that triggered it all. Yes, the walking and the accomplishments that follow are of our own doing. Yet it is that brief contact with something greater, kinder, and wiser that starts the journey that changes our lives. It is that spark, that new knowledge that awakens us to the possibility that life and the world can be different than what we have experienced until then. In that moment, we begin to break free from the mental traps we have either built for ourselves or accepted from others—constraining ideas about what life should be like, what success should be like, what happiness should be like—and gather the courage to go find our own definitions.

It is that nudge, that insight from the Light, that awakens us from a life of dissatisfaction that cannot culminate in anything but the slow death of our happiness. Without constant reflection and an active search for meaning and purpose in our lives, we can fall into the morose slumber of everyday life. If we are not attentive, we begin to think only of our immediate responsibilities and desires, often neglecting our higher needs. We wake up in the morning and rush to drop the kids at school or beat that daily rush-hour traffic then we go to work so we can pay rent or make those mortgage payments; and later we dash to the grocery store before returning home to catch that TV show or take care of that one more thing in our to-do list before falling asleep. Then we repeat it the next day, and the next, and the next... All of these things are important, no doubt, and need to happen. But if we forget why we do all of these to begin with and find little to no joy in them, days blur into weeks that blend into months. Suddenly years have gone by and it seems like you have been in one long slumber, like we have been asleep and can only recall hazy memories of time gone by, as if in a dream without a proper storyline or purpose. If that is where we find ourselves, then there may be little difference between our lives and those unrecognizable zombies in the TV shows, movies, and books popping up everywhere. Fortunately, we are not fated to eat brains for breakfast nor to roam aimlessly forever in walking-dead status: we can awaken from that state. And all it takes is us wanting different—or a little push off our everyday horses...

THE SHINING LIGHT:

"Awake, you that sleep, and arise from the dead, and Christ will shine on you."
(Ephesians 5:14)

Perhaps that is one way to understand Paul's words to the group of seekers in Ephesus, Turkey, who sought his advice two thousand years ago. In that one statement he shared his own journey with them, rolling into one powerful sentence his incredible transformation from Saul to Paul and how much brighter life was for him after this change—how he had awakened from the sleep of the world to a new life filled with purpose and understanding, where he more clearly saw his role in the cosmos.

Interestingly, Paul leaves space in the statement for multiple ways of awakening to this greater reality. He does not prescribe or impose how the transformation should take place—he only says that when it does, we will be met with a light that will shine on us from somewhere very high: the Christ. And what is the Christ? The word may be loaded with added religious meaning today, but given the context of the time, the Christ was the Jewish messiah, the anointed liberator who would come to free the people. And that is exactly what happened to Paul: through an encounter with the Christ, his process of liberation from the expectations and social constructs Saul had created or taken upon himself began. Because his own process was never forced upon him, Paul would not force that on others either. The Light of the Christ may have barged in, but it never imposed; it just asked and supported. Paul would do the same: he would invite, but never force. He would sound the clarion[2] to the world about this greater reality, but not violate one of the greatest proofs of God's love for us: free will. To read into his actions or words any sense of coercion is to misunderstand the process of liberation altogether—or to read text and teachings that are not his.

So, it is up to us to determine how we will embark on this transformation, how we will turn the lights on. Whether we consciously seek it ourselves (which is rare) or whether life will give us a push before we dig ourselves an even deeper spiritual or emotional hole (which is more common), the good news is that the end result is the same: enlightenment. Happiness. We all can get there. That is the timeless reassurance coming from the Light above.

Paul needed a push. We may as well. The push may seem painful at first, but with time we come to value it— or, rather, the Light behind it. For Paul, it was the little-known prophet from Nazareth called Jesus who showed himself to Saul on the road and pointed to a different way of being. For us, it is not much different: it is that same Jesus who calls us to reconsider the way we go about our lives. The crucial difference here is that Paul's Jesus is not always the Jesus we have come to know today in mainstream culture. Something happened during the two thousand years that separate us from Paul that has led us to separate ourselves from the essence of Jesus and of that for which he stood.

The prophet Paul came to know was a game-changer who spoke of tolerance and love (because they are the same thing, at different levels); who sought out those in deepest need to bring them comfort; who accepted and engaged with everyone, even those excluded by the status quo and those who wished to bring him down; who sat with people, broke bread with them, answered their questions, and told them stories of hope and this world's transience in ways they could understand. That was a Jesus who knew our shortcomings, accepted them, and remained close to us even when we would betray the very high ideals he stood for; a Jesus who humbled himself washing our feet so we would learn of the importance of service to others; a Jesus who did not care much for worldly possessions or worry about the number of followers he had; one who really lived the ideas and concepts he shared every day; and, ultimately, a Jesus who did what no other figure has done since then: show us that there is life after this one and that we need not be as afraid of death. No wonder that Jesus split history into before and after Him.

Contrast that to the Jesus some of our churches and Christians tell us of today. Through their words and actions, they put forth a Jesus who chooses some groups over others; a Jesus who points fingers at those who may be different; a Jesus who only speaks in extremes and is unforgiving; a Jesus who gives people ultimatums about how to live, and who would deny rights to those who don't follow them; a Jesus who suggests we should smite our "enemies" instead of loving them; who says material abundance is something to be aspired to as a sign of divine favor; a Jesus who prefers large, luxurious houses of worship over personal conversations and assistance to those who struggle; and even a Jesus who has opinions about elections... This is a different Jesus than the one Paul encountered two millennia ago. This "new" Jesus resembles more the oppressive leaders who persecuted him and the Caesars of the time, who were more concerned with keeping power within specific circles than educating and serving those they led. "Status-quo Jesus" and "game-changer Jesus" are not the same: two thousand years and major philosophical differences separate them, like oil and water.

If Paul had met "status-quo Jesus" on the road to Damascus, chances are he would still be Saul. After all, that was exactly what Saul stood for: the maintaining of "tradition" and of power over others instead of power over self. So, when we think of the light the Christ brings us in Paul's message to the Ephesians, let us be clear about what Christ we are talking about—and what Christ he was talking about. You too will have to choose your Jesus—or, put another way, your take on the messages from the Creator of All Things. The Christ we call forth into our daily lives must be the nondenominational and all accepting messiah who speaks of and supports personal transformation as the only means to change and happiness —because it is through experience, through living the changes we want to see in the world, that we are made fulfilled. After all, it is truth that sets us free, that liberates us—not other people. It will not be our churches, pastors, gurus, priests, guides, coaches, or friends who will walk our road for us: it will be us, with our own two feet, one heart, and one mind.

So, as we walk our own ways on the road of life and continually rediscover what we want and who we want to be, let us also pierce the veil that covers what is above us guiding us through it all. The assurance that there is something greater and all-loving guiding us can transform our attitudes toward everything in and around ourselves. It can instill in our hearts that sense of security we need to move forward, which we cannot always find in others or in the world around us. It can sustain us when we falter. It can inspire us when we waver. That is why the Light was so important to Paul—why it helped him continue on his journey. It can do the same for us too. Even if everything else we pondered about so far was about Paul's journey and the act of walking the road, it all started with that brief encounter with the Light. Without that spark, that initial message from Above passed on by the ultimate messenger of the Divine, Christ (the Liberator), Paul's journey would have lasted much longer—perhaps many more lifetimes. That may help explain why his impactful message to his friends in Ephesus—and to us—contained such strong imagery: because the contrast between Saul and Paul was profound, like night and day. And so was the difference in personal fulfillment between Saul's and Paul's experiences. That is what lies ahead for us too.

Hence the timeless invitation that is extended to us today. Propelled by that Light, let's put aside the old versions of ourselves that no longer suit us and our preconceived notions that no longer serve us, like Paul had to put Saul aside somewhere between Jerusalem and Damascus. The price of change is letting go. The reward for changing is the infinite ahead of us. The choice is always ours.

May you awaken from the unsatisfying sleep the world offers us, take your future into your own hands with the certainty that a new and better life lies before you, and find the lasting light of personal satisfaction, fulfillment, and growth that comes from discovering and meeting your purpose in this life and beyond. And may you, in turn, shine your light onto others walking along the road in search of meaning and purpose in this life.

The open road lies ahead. Shall we follow it?

ACKNOWLEDGMENTS

No journey happens in isolation. Although each one of us must walk our own road, we are always made better by the company and kindness of others along the way. To that end, I would like to thank the many people who have made a difference in my life — and who are too numerous to name here — and those who were specially supportive of the creation of this book.

To my wife, Nicole, gratitude for the unwavering support that allows me to embrace projects and travel that take time away from family. Nothing I do would be possible without you. It is as simple as that.

Thanks also to Hannah Kushnick, whose brilliance and razor sharp linguistic skills help me distill the writing to the clearest and simplest form I can muster. And to André Magalhães for catching the typos, extra spaces, and missing words that escaped three other people. Almost 30 years later and you are still patiently helping me. Thank you.

And to my Life Forward team, you also make it into the book! Alejandro Martin, Steve McKenney, Kanika Raney, Pat Lynch, Debi Hemmeter, and Laurie "Elle" Finnegan, thank you for helping me get to the finish line. Elle, a big thank you for being such a champion for the book! It is humbling to hear from many people who reached out because you told them they had to read it. Funny how it is often the person who writes the book who learns the most from it...

Finally, thank you to the incredible examples of selfless dedication and noble character I have encountered throughout my entire life: teachers, mentors, family members, coaches, friends... I may not have learned all the lessons I could or should have, but I know I am better because of your example. Thank you especially to Divaldo Franco and Joanna de Angelis, whose presence has certainly changed my life for the better. And, finally, thank you to Paul and Jesus, both of whom I have learned to know anew. Removing the patina of old religious thinking applied by others to their teachings has allowed me to never feel alone again — in this life or in the many more to come. What else can one possibly ask for?

ABOUT THE AUTHOR

Dan Assisi, Ed.D., MPA, PMP, is an award-winning author and internationally celebrated speaker who has delivered hundreds of talks and workshops on spirituality in over 60 cities in 4 continents. Known for a mix of deep thinking and witty humor, Dan takes a unique approach to spirituality that is steeped in reason to remind audiences everywhere of our spiritual nature.

Dr. Assisi is a founding member of The Spiritist Institute and was featured in the Togetherness Video Series, an interfaith documentary on religious diversity and spirituality. You can also find him as the host of the Spiritist Conversations podcast.

Daniel is an executive coach and strategy consultant to nonprofit organizations. His portfolio of clients include national and state-wide organizations focusing on innovation and on reimagining the public education space. Daniel holds a Doctorate degree in Education and a Masters in Public Administration with a Graduate Certificate in Public Policy from the University of Southern California. He is also a credentialed Project Management Professional.

If he could, Dan would spend his life reading and traveling. Meanwhile, he lives in San Diego with his wife Nicole and his two sons, where he is diligently testing the idea that one can never be overexposed to blue skies, palm trees, and the ocean.

Website: www.danassisi.com
(Sign up for my monthly newsletter!)

facebook.com/DanAssisi

instagram.com/DanAssisi

twitter.com/DanAssisi

goodreads.com/DanAssisi

youtube.com/DanAssisi

COPYRIGHT PERMISSIONS

DISCUSSION QUESTIONS

1. *Our Road to Damascus* opens with a quote from Paul's *Letter to the Ephesians*: "Awake, you that sleep, and arise from the dead, and Christ will shine on you." (Ephesians 5:14) Toward the end of the book, the author returns to this passage. Why do you think he chose it to frame this book? Did your interpretation of the passage change after reading the book? Why or why not?

2. In "Lesson 1: In a Group But Alone", the author writes that one of the key lessons we must learn in our lives is how to cope with loss. He further makes a distinction between losing people physical and emotionally. Which one is harder for you and why? Later, he makes the argument that, if we take a higher vantage point and focus on what we have gained from these relationships, we will never truly lose anyone. Have you been able to shift your perspective

from loss to gratitude in your life? Is your current mindset a "glass half-empty" or a "glass half-full" one? If not, what would it take for you to make the leap?

3. Dan argues that opportunities for meaningful change frequently present themselves at difficult moments in our lives in "Lesson 2: A Destabilizing Moment". In retrospect, what curveballs has life thrown at you that have helped you grow in ways you would not have otherwise? How would you be different today if they did not present themselves to you?

4. Personal transformation requires a good deal of self-reflection. In "Lesson 3: The Courageous Question," the author talks about conviction and comfort as two key aspects of decision-making. How often do you find yourself motivated by comfort over conviction? What are some examples of how your life has changed because of decisions you made out of conviction? How would your life be different 5 or 10 years from now if you were able to prioritize conviction over comfort in your decision-making?

5. In "Lesson 4: The Temporary Blindness" the author introduces us to the concept of a symbolic "Damascene blindness". Have you experienced temporary confusion about your purpose or place in life as a result of a transformative experience? If so, how did you navigate the uncertainty? If you could go back in

time, what advice would you give your younger self about weathering difficult moments?

6. The author imagines a group of thinkers sitting together for a conversation with Paul at the end of "Lesson 5: The Decision to Go Ahead". If you could pick a spot to sit at that table, would you sit beside Lev Vygotsky, Carol Dweck or T.S. Eliot? Why? What would you talk to them about?

7. "Lesson 6: The Unexpected Help" reminds us that we always receive a helping hand from the universe when we are engaged in noble pursuits. In Saul's case, it came from where he least expected: Ananias. What are some moments in your life when you received "unexpected help"? If so, who or what was your Ananias?

8. In "Lesson 7: A Different Damascus", the author makes a case for the use of guiding principles rather than particular objectives as our north stars in life. He argues that "a guiding principle approach trains us to refocus our minds from the chasing of the specific and shallow to the pursuit of the inspirational and more profound." What are the guiding principles that have led you to where you are today? More importantly, what guiding principles will you choose to reach your Damascus?

9. At the beginning of the book, the author says there is a lot of confusion about "religion", which he calls a "loaded word". He goes on to

state this book "is not a religious one in the sense of organized religion." He then takes the time to differentiate between religion—which he calls an "individual sport"—and organized religion—which he describes as "rules, practices and guidelines" that came about from people's effort to come together to study religion in groups. Ultimately, he argues for the use of the first lens and develops the entire book accordingly. How would this book have been different if he had chosen the perspective of organized religion as a lens? Which lens do you use to interpret and understand the teachings of Jesus?

10. *Our Road to Damascus* is a book about personal transformation. Personal transformation, the author argues, starts with an encounter with the "Light"—important new information that calls us to change our perspective. In his encounter with the "Light", Saul was asked why he was persecuting the ideas the Christ brought forth. If you had your own encounter with the "Light" today, what do you think it would tell you?

APPENDIX: PEOPLE MENTIONED IN THE BOOK

Below is a list (in alphabetical order by first name) of some of the people cited throughout the book. For context, a brief biographical description from Wikipedia is also included. (Biblical figures were not included in this list.) It is the author's hope it may inspire you to get to know their works in more detail.

Allan Kardec is the nom de plume of the French educator, translator and author Hippolyte Léon Denizard Rivail (3 October 1804 – 31 March 1869). He is the author of the five books known as the Spiritist Codification, and is the founder of Spiritism.

Benjamin Franklin FRS FRSA FRSE (January 17, 1706– April 17, 1790) was an American polymath and one of the Founding Fathers of the United States. Franklin was a leading writer, printer, political philosopher, politician, Freemason, postmaster, scientist, inventor, humorist, civic activist, statesman, and diplomat. As a scientist, he was a major figure in the American Enlightenment and the history of physics for his discoveries and theories regarding electricity. As an inventor, he is known for the lightning rod, bifocals, and the Franklin stove, among other inventions. He founded many civic organizations, including the Library Company, Philadelphia's first fire department, and the University of Pennsylvania.

Carol Susan Dweck (born October 17, 1946) is an American psychologist. She is the Lewis and Virginia Eaton Professor of Psychology at Stanford University. Dweck is known for her work on the mindset psychological trait. She taught at Columbia University, Harvard University, and the University of Illinois before joining the Stanford University faculty in 2004. She is a Fellow of the Association for Psychological Science.

Charles Lutwidge Dodgson (27 January 1832 – 14 January 1898), better known by his pen name Lewis Carroll, was an English writer of children's fiction, notably Alice's Adventures in Wonderland and its sequel Through the Looking-Glass. He was noted for his facility at word play, logic, and fantasy. He was also a mathematician, photographer, inventor and Anglican deacon.

Elisabeth Kübler-Ross (July 8, 1926 – August 24, 2004) was a Swiss-American psychiatrist, a pioneer in near-death studies, and author of the internationally best-selling book, On Death and Dying (1969), where she first discussed her theory of the five stages of grief, also known as the "Kübler-Ross model".

Heraclitus of Ephesus (c. 535 – c. 475 BC) was an Ancient Greek, pre-Socratic, Ionian philosopher and a native of the city of Ephesus, which was then part of the Persian Empire. His appreciation for wordplay and oracular expressions, as well as paradoxical elements in his philosophy, earned him the epithet "The Obscure" from antiquity. He wrote a single work, *On Nature*, only fragments of which have survived, increasing the obscurity associated with his life and philosophy.

Jean Piaget (9 August 1896 – 16 September 1980) was a Swiss psychologist known for his work on child development. Piaget's 1936 theory of cognitive development and epistemological view are together called "genetic epistemology".

John Donne (22 January 1572[1] – 31 March 1631) was an English poet, scholar, soldier and secretary born into a Catholic family, a remnant of the Catholic Revival, who reluctantly became a cleric in the Church of England. He was Dean of St Paul's Cathedral in London (1621–1631). He is considered the pre-eminent representative of the metaphysical poets. His poetical works are noted for their metaphorical and sensual style and include sonnets, love poems, religious poems, Latin translations, epigrams, elegies, songs, and satires. He is also known for his sermons.

Lev Semyonovich Vygotsky (November 17, 1896 – June 11, 1934) was a Soviet psychologist, known for his work on psychological development in children. He published on a diverse range of subjects, and from multiple views as his perspective changed over the years. Among his students was Alexander Luria.

Louis Daniel Armstrong (August 4, 1901 – July 6, 1971), nicknamed "Satchmo", "Satch", and "Pops", was an American trumpeter, composer, vocalist, and actor who was among the most influential figures in jazz. His career spanned five decades, from the 1920s to the 1960s, and different eras in the history of jazz. In 2017, he was inducted into the Rhythm & Blues Hall of Fame.

Siddhārtha Gautama (also known as the Buddha) was a philosopher, mendicant, meditator, spiritual teacher, and religious leader who lived in Ancient India (c. 5th to 4th century BCE). He is revered as the founder of the world religion of Buddhism, and worshipped by most Buddhist schools as the Enlightened One who has transcended Karma and escaped the cycle of birth and rebirth. He taught for around 45 years and built a large following, both monastic and lay. His teaching is based on his insight into duḥkha (typically translated as "suffering") and the end of dukkha – the state called Nibbāna or Nirvana.

Thomas Stearns Eliot OM (26 September 1888 – 4 January 1965) was an American-born British poet, essayist, publisher, playwright, literary critic and editor. Born in St. Louis, Missouri, to a prominent Boston Brahmin family, he moved to England in 1914 at the age of 25 and went on to settle, work and marry there. He became a British subject in 1927 at the age of 39, subsequently renouncing his American citizenship. Eliot is considered one of the 20th century's major poets.

NOTES

2. WHY PAUL?

1. The word gospel is derived from the Anglo-Saxon term god-spell, meaning "good story," a rendering of the Latin evangelium and the Greek euangelion, meaning "good news" or "good telling."
   Encyclopaedia Britannica, s.v. "Gospel." Encyclopaedia Britannica, 2018. https://www.britannica.com/topic/Gospel-New-Testament (accessed November 21, 2020).

2. As a quick aside, that also serves to explain why Paul may sometimes sound less accepting in some texts than he surely was: with time, his letters may have been "bent" or modified by careless scribes who copied everything into the next Bible they were producing, including comments on the margins from someone else that ended up finding their way into canonical text as if they were Paul's; or by scholars wishing to leverage Paul's credibility to push forth their own personal agenda. An example is the "woman must be silent in church" passage on chapter 14 of the first letter to Corinthians: nothing is more unlike Paul than comments like that. At any rate, impersonation or adulteration of his writings only happened because Paul was so significant.

3. Hackett, Conrad, and David McClendon. "Fact tank: Christians remain world's largest religious group, but they are declining in Europe." Pew Research Center. April 5, 2017. https://www.pewresearch.org/fact-tank/2017/04/05/christians-remain-worlds-largest-religious-group-but-they-are-declining-in-europe.

4. Naturally, this was less of a focus for Jews who had begun to pay more and more attention to the teachings of this unlikely prophet from poor Nazareth. For them, perhaps the biggest hurdle was reconciling their expectations of what the promised messiah would be like with the type of person the historical Jesus was. Scripture seemed to point to the coming of a prince of the world, and most Jews probably expected a prophet that would also gain political control over the affairs of the chosen people to lead them to a leadership role over all nations. It may bear saying that separation of state and church, something normal and expected in contemporary

Western nation-states, was not necessarily sought after at the time by the children of Abraham. Instead, they got a poor carpenter from the unfashionable region of Galilee who shied away from political power, entered Jerusalem on a donkey, and suffered the death reserved for the worst of criminals: crucifixion. To qualify that as a bummer would perhaps be to say it nicely. For Jews of the time, accepting Jesus as the heralded messiah meant bursting big bubbles of expectation already. But, hey, at least Jesus was Jewish.

3. THE STORY

1. Guinness World Records. Best-selling book. Accessed November 2, 2020. https://www.guinnessworldrecords.com/world-records/best-selling-book-of-non-fiction.
2. And if that is interesting to you, then we should also mention scholars see the Acts of the Apostles as the continuation of the Gospel of Luke and believe the same author wrote both—even if they are unsure if it really was Luke. History aside, this is not an argument by authority: I mention it here so you know where to find it, if your curiosity is piqued. Regardless of authorship, the value of the story remains.

    We also find mentions of Paul's experience in First Corinthians and in Galatians—letters attributed to Paul written to the early Christian communities in Corinth (Greece) and Galatia (modern-day Turkey), respectively. They are brief references, however, so for brevity we leave them aside in favor of what we find in Acts.
3. Acts 9:1-19
4. Acts 22:6
5. Acts 9:4
6. Acts 22:8, Acts 9:5
7. Acts 22:10
8. Acts 22:11
9. Acts 9:11
10. Acts 9:9
11. Acts 9:10
12. Acts 9:18

5. LESSON 1: IN A GROUP BUT ALONE

1. Xavier, Francisco Cândido. *Paul and Stephen*. FEB Publisher; 2019.
2. Xavier, Francisco Cândido. *Paul and Stephen*. FEB Editora; 2019.
3. Acts 9:11
4. Xavier, Francisco Cândido. *Paul and Stephen*. FEB Publisher; 2019.
5. Matthew 6:20 (ESV)
6. Antoine de Saint-Exupéry's *Little Prince* comes to mind here.

6. LESSON 2: A DESTABILIZING MOMENT

1. Acts 22:6

7. LESSON 3: THE COURAGEOUS QUESTION

1. Acts 22:10
2. Acts 22:10
3. Acts 9:4
4. Acts 22:8, Acts 9:5
5. Acts 22:10
6. Acts 22:10
7. Acts 22:7-10
8. See T.S. Eliot's poem "The Love Song of J. Alfred Prufrock."
9. Acts 22:10

8. LESSON 4: THE TEMPORARY BLINDNESS

1. Dweck, Carol S. *Mindset: The New Psychology of Success*. New York: Random House, 2006.
2. Totally a side note: for an interesting analysis of leadership through different generations, read Bennis and Thomas's *Geeks and Geezers*.
   Bennis, Warren G, and Robert J. Thomas. *Geeks & Geezers: How*

Era, Values, and Defining Moments Shape Leaders. Boston: Harvard Business School Press, 2002. Print.

9. LESSON 5: THE DECISION TO GO AHEAD

1. Eliot, T S. *Four Quartets*. England: Gramophone Co, 1950. Sound recording.
2. Yes, I am well aware I totally dated myself there.

10. LESSON 6: THE UNEXPECTED HELP

1. Xavier, Francisco Cândido. *Paul and Stephen*. FEB Publisher; 2019.
2. Acts 9:9
3. Acts 9:10
4. Acts 9:18
5. 1 Corinthians 13:4-8
6. Acts 9:11
7. Acts 9:2
8. See John Donne's "Meditation XVII: Devotions upon Emergent Occasions."
   Donne, John, and C A. Patrides. *The Complete English Poems of John Donne*. London: Dent, 1985. Print.

11. LESSON 7: A DIFFERENT DAMASCUS

1. See the April 1861 issue of Allan Kardec's *The Spiritist Review*.
   Kardec, Allan. 1861. The Spiritist review: Journal of Psychological Studies.
2. Rediger, Jeffrey. *Cured: The Life-Changing Science of Spontaneous Healing*. New York: Flatiron, 2020.
3. Sison, Gerardo. "Does your body really replace itself every 7 years?" *Discovery*, August 1, 2019. https://www.discovery.com/science/Body-Really-Replace-Itself-Every-7-Years.
4. Lipka, Michael, and Claire Gegewicz. "More Americans now say they're spiritual but not religious." Pew Research Center. September 6, 2017. https://www.pewresearch.org/fact-

tank/2017/09/06/more-americans-now-say-theyre-spiritual-but-not-religious.

5. Carroll, Lewis. *Alice's Adventures in Wonderland*. New York: Macmillan, 1920.

12. OUR ROAD TO DAMASCUS AND BEYOND

1. Galatians 1:17
2. See Thomas Osbert Mordaunt's poem *The Call*:
   "Sound, sound the clarion, fill the fife!
   Throughout the sensual world proclaim,
   One crowded hour of glorious life
   Is worth an age without a name."
   Quiller-Couch, Arthur Thomas. 2018. *The Oxford book of English verse, 1250-1900*. Oxford: Clarendon Press. http://online.canadiana.ca/view/oocihm.65179.

REFERENCE LIST

Bennis, Warren G, and Robert J. Thomas. *Geeks & Geezers: How Era, Values, and Defining Moments Shape Leaders*. Boston: Harvard Business School Press, 2002.

Carroll, Lewis. *Alice's Adventures in Wonderland*. New York: Macmillan, 1920.

Donne, John, and C. A. Patrides. *The Complete English Poems of John Donne*. London: Dent, 1985. Print.

Dweck, Carol S. *Mindset: The New Psychology of Success*. New York: Random House, 2006. Print.

Eliot, T S. *Four Quartets*. England: Gramophone Co, 1950. Sound recording.

Eliot, T. S. "The Love Song of J. Alfred Prufrock." *Gleeditions*, 17 Apr. 2011, www.gleeditions.com/alfred-prufrock/students/pages.asp?lid=303&pg=7. Originally published in *Poetry: A Magazine of Verse*, June 1915, pp. 130-135.

Kardec, Allan. 1861. *The Spiritist review: Journal of Psychological Studies.*

Kardec, Allan. *The Gospel according to spiritism.* Edicei of America, 2011. Print.

Lipka, Michael, and Claire Gegewicz. "More Americans now say they're spiritual but not religious." Pew Research Center. September 6, 2017. https://www.pewresearch.org/fact-tank/2017/09/06/more-americans-now-say-theyre-spiritual-but-not-religious.

Quiller-Couch, Arthur Thomas. 2018. *The Oxford book of English verse, 1250-1900.* Oxford: Clarendon Press. http://online.canadiana.ca/view/oocihm.65179.

Rediger, Jeffrey. *Cured: The Life-Changing Science of Spontaneous Healing.* New York: Flatiron, 2020. Print.

Saint-Exupéry, Antoine de, and Katherine Woods. *The Little Prince.* Harcourt Brace Jovanovich, 1961. Print.

Sison, Gerardo. "Does your body really replace itself every 7 years?" *Discovery*, August 1, 2019. https://www.discovery.com/science/Body-Really-Replace-Itself-Every-7-Years.

Xavier, Francisco Cândido. *Paul and Stephen*. FEB Publisher; 2019. Print.

ENJOYED THIS BOOK?

Word of mouth and reader reviews remain the best way new books and new authors get exposure.

If you enjoyed the unique perspective *Our Road to Damascus* brings to an old story, please consider sharing it with family, friends, and colleagues.

Please also consider ratings this book on Amazon, Goodreads, the Apple Store, the Google Store, and everywhere else books are sold. It helps!

Thank you for your readership.

To keep up-to-date with Dan's future projects, join his monthly newsletter at www.danassisi.com.